Praise for

Scripture First

"Olden and Stark have assembled six powerful essays firmly grounded in Old and New Testament depictions of God's people striving to understand God's word. Rather than the divisive patternistic restorationism often used in Churches of Christ, the authors convincingly advocate methods of interpreting Scripture that focus on the core affirmations of Christian faith—especially those proclaimed at and embodied in baptism. The object of godly biblical interpretation is the formation of the church into the image of Christ. These authors provide perhaps the healthiest and most hopeful way forward toward this goal seen today in Churches of Christ."

—**Douglas A. Foster,** University Scholar in Residence, Abilene Christian University

"These essays spark creative thought regarding how biblical interpretation impacts Christian unity. While focused on those related to the Stone-Campbell movement, the authors' analyses of texts and methods can benefit those in a much wider circle. A good read for anyone meditating on the concept of a rule of faith and its role in understanding Scripture and building up the body of Christ."

—**Susan Bubbers,** Dean, The Center for Anglican Theology

"*Scripture First* calls us to consider what it means to take Scripture seriously. The authors prompt us to avoid blindly accepting or quickly rejecting the Restoration Movement principle of finding unity through adherence to Scripture. This work is challenging and thought-provoking; and, hopefully, it will spark significant conversations within the Stone-Campbell Movement and outside it as well."

—**Todd Brenneman,** Professor of Christian History, Faulkner University

"The Restoration Movement was birthed from a holy desire to unify divided Christian communities under the authority of sacred Scripture. While some hermeneutical commitments evinced in the movement have proven insufficient for that lofty goal, recent historical and theological work and increasing self-awareness have made possible new interpretive vistas that are critically and faithfully grounded in the achievements of Christian forebears—both Restorationists and others. These essays exhibit the best characteristics of such work. My hope is that *Scripture First* will be read widely to the edification and gentle provocation of all still committed to sharing in the mysterious work of the Father, reconciling all things in heaven and on earth in the Son through the Holy Spirit."

—**Joseph K. Gordon,** Associate Professor of Theology, Johnson University

"*Scripture First* calls for a new kind of patternism. Grounded in a close reading of Scripture, the authors recognize the core affirmations of the faith, promote the historic confession of those affirmations, and call for their expression in both liturgy and communal reading. This project faithfully reads Scripture and offers a path toward a fuller embodiment of the visible unity of the body of Christ. The integration of Scripture, the great tradition of the church, and a living community is, as Thomas Campbell speculated there might be, a 'better way' to realize unity in the present."

—**John Mark Hicks,** Professor of Theology, Lipscomb University

SCRIPTURE FIRST

SCRIPTURE FIRST

Biblical Interpretation That Fosters Christian Unity

Edited By

Daniel B. Oden & J. David Stark

FOREWORD BY MARK W. HAMILTON

SCRIPTURE FIRST

Biblical Interpretation That Fosters Christian Unity

ISBN 978-1-68426-091-1 | LCCN 2020015870

Printed in the United States of America

LIBRARY OF CONGRESS CATALOGING-IN-PUBLICATION DATA
Names: Oden, Daniel B., editor. | Stark, J. David, editor.
Title: Scripture first : biblical interpretation that fosters Christian unity / Daniel B. Oden, and J. David Stark.
Description: Abilene, Texas : Abilene Christian University Press , 2020. | Includes bibliographical references and index.
Identifiers: LCCN 2020015870 | ISBN 9781684260911 (paperback) | ISBN 9781684269501 (epub)
Subjects: LCSH: Bible—Evidences, authority, etc. | Bible and tradition. | Bible—Criticism, interpretation, etc. | Tradition (Theology) | Authority—Religious aspects—Christianity.
Classification: LCC BS480 .S348 2020 | DDC 220.1—dc23
LC record available at https://lccn.loc.gov/2020015870

Cover design by Thinkpen Design | Interior text design by Sandy Armstrong, Strong Design

For information contact:
Abilene Christian University Press
ACU Box 29138, Abilene, Texas 79699

1-877-816-4455 | www.acupressbooks.com

20 21 22 23 24 25 / 7 6 5 4 3 2 1

Contents

FOREWORD

Mark W. Hamilton

In the introduction to his translation of the Vulgate, John Wyclif pointed to the horizons of biblical interpretation, landmarking both the character of the reader and the divine purposes for human beings. Signaling the need to read the Bible in multilayered ways appropriate both to its nature and the readers' needs, he wrote:

> Whatever thing in God's word may not be referred properly to seemliness of virtues or to the truth of faith, it is figurative speech. Seemliness of virtues pertains to love God and the neighbor; truth of faith pertains to know God and the neighbor. Holy Scripture commands nothing but charity, it blames nothing but illicit desire, and in that manner, it informs the virtues or good conditions of men. Holy Scripture affirms nothing but Christian faith by things past, present, and to come, and

> all these things pertain to nourish charity, and make it strong, and to overcome and quench illicit desire.[1]

In other words, the church reads the Bible with a view toward the spiritual and intellectual encounter with God, as well as relationships with other human beings. Doctrine and life closely relate as sound teaching quenches the soul's squalid attempts to master others and use them for its own purposes. No biblical interpretation should aid the movement away from virtue—that is, away from the God who gave the word in the first place.

The authors of the present book stand in a line descending directly from Wyclif's work from six centuries ago. All free-church Protestants do. Despite his intentions, the "morning star of the Reformation" has begotten a galaxy, of which the Churches of Christ comprise a small but shiny constellation. Yet, too often, we have reduced (or traduced) the Bible to a blueprint for church structure, its specifications not so much shining forth in the plain sense of the stories, laws, poems, and prophecies making up the bulk of Holy Writ as tucked away in inferences drawn from snippets cut and pasted together to justify a pattern that has emerged in the interpreter's mind. At our best, we have celebrated the power of obedience through concrete acts of service. At our worst, we

---

[1] Wyclif's original text in late Middle English is available in John Wyclif, "The Wycliffite Bible: From the Prologue," in *Medieval English Political Writings*, ed. James M. Dean, Middle English Texts (Kalamazoo, MI: Teaching Association for Medieval Studies [TEAMS], 1996), 61. The text there runs,

> Whatever thing in Goddis word may not be referrid propirly to onesté of vertues neither to the treuthe of feith, it is figuratyf speche. Onestee of vertues perteyneth to love God and the neighebore; treuthe of faith perteyneth to knowe God and the neighebore. Hooly Scripture comaundith no thing no but charité, it blamith no thing no but coveitise; and in that manere it enfoormeth the vertues either goode condiscouns of men. Holy Scripture affermith no thing no but Cristen feith bi thingis passid, present, and to comynge, and alle these things perteynen to nursche charité, and make it strong, and to overcome and quenche coveitise.

For readability, I have given the text above in a modern English translation.

have substituted works' righteousness for the more radical path of trust in the God who saves—and reveals.

Over the past four decades, biblical scholars, theologians, and preachers in Churches of Christ have increasingly rejected the patternism, prooftexting, and legalism of our immediate past. Sometimes this liberation came through historical criticism, the careful examination of the literary shaping of the biblical text in its earliest recoverable settings of creation and reception. Sometimes it came through attention to the spiritual disciplines, both individual and congregational. And sometimes it came out of nausea at the ever-intensifying odors of legalism, with its endless efforts at purging all "false teachers" whose views deviated ever so slightly from the groupthink of the powers that aspired to be. Whatever its sources, change has occurred.

Yet, as many have discovered, helping our nonbeliefs is much easier than living by our beliefs. As the authors of this volume make clear, if we want to read the Bible more fully, we must do more than identify what we no longer think. We must attend to a careful exegesis of both the biblical text and the work of the community of readers as it lives with that text over time. Attempts to return to the New Testament (or the Bible as a whole) as though it objectively described a world beyond history and culture are doomed to fail because they rest on false assumptions about the text and the readers. Primitivist restorationism ignores the literary genres of the Bible, the history of its creation and canonization, and the further substantive history of its reception in formal theology, sermons, and the arts. Primitivist restorationism is an exercise in pretending that Scripture differs greatly from its true nature. And primitivist restorationism invites division, as it invests one person's or group's interpretation with the prestige of the ancient church itself.

Still, something of the old instincts remains relevant. Valuable parts of the legacy of Churches of Christ include (1) a commitment to close reading of the biblical text; (2) a sense that the text matters in some ultimate way to the lives of individuals and communities because it bears witness to God, not just to human experiences of a given time and place; and (3) the belief that the church as a whole is a proper reader of the biblical text, not just scholars or individual pious Christians.

The authors of this work address these themes with skill and courage. They engage the Bible itself with great care, identifying ways in which the writers of Scripture set their words within the larger context of core Christian confessions of God's saving work through Jesus Christ. The longstanding idea that Scripture must be understood in light of the church's life as a saved people is put forward afresh through careful exegesis of the Bible's own creedal consciousness. Several contributors remind us that the sharp distinction between creed and Scripture does not appear in the Bible itself.

They also remind us that the Bible is most at home not in debates about ever-narrower points of congregational practice but in the life of worship and deeds of service. And in so arguing, they show themselves profoundly loyal to the core commitments of Churches of Christ. As Thomas Campbell expressed those commitments more than two centuries ago, "were it possible, we would also desire to adopt and recommend such measures, as would give rest to our brethren throughout all the churches;—as would restore unity, peace, and purity, to the whole church of God."[2] While Campbell's biblical minimalism has not delivered the results he hoped for, his theological generosity and desire for truth amid the haze of opinion and human striving still resonate today. They certainly do in this volume.

---

[2]Thomas Campbell, "Declaration and Address," in *The Quest for Christian Unity, Peace, and Purity in Thomas Campbell's* Declaration and Address: *Text and Studies*, ed. Thomas H. Olbricht and Hans Rollmann, ATLA Monograph Series 46 (Lanham, MD: Scarecrow, 2000), 3.

Finally, any proposal for interpreting Scripture ought to be logically coherent, responsive to the long history of biblical interpretation and reflection thereon, and able to account for the biblical text we have rather than some imaginary, more pristine text. Such a proposal ought to help form a community that is both historically conscious and spiritually sensitive. The central work of biblical interpretation ought to be identifying how biblical texts think about humanity before God. Questions of textual origins, the stuff of technical exegesis, and the like should not disappear but should serve the higher purpose of understanding how the biblical texts dealt with successive, interlocking problems raised by the ongoing Israelite, Jewish, and Christian encounter with the God of Moses and Jesus.

Not only must any theory of biblical inspiration, authority, or usage account for the sort of text the Bible is (as the failure to do so causes fundamentalist proposals to fail), but proposals for reconstructing the history of the text must account for it as a theological document in a robust sense. The authors of this book blaze compatible paths toward such an accounting. For that, we owe them a great debt of gratitude, best repaid through ongoing discussion, teaching, and prayer.

Introduction

Daniel B. Oden and J. David Stark

From very early in its heritage, the American Restoration Movement articulated two core principles: unity among Christians and the use of Scripture alone as Christians' authority for faith and practice.[1] In emphasizing the latter, the Restoration Movement amplified the European Reformation's rejection of church tradition. As a function of their emphasis on Scripture alone, Stone-Campbell fellowships have regularly defined "tradition" (e.g., councils, creeds, confessions, catechisms) as antithetical to Scripture.

Scripture is of divine origin; tradition is wholly human. Scripture is wholly truthful; tradition can be wrong and likely

[1]Greg Sterling reaffirmed and called for restoration heirs to maintain these distinctive emphases in his plenary address "Memory, Tradition, and the Future of Faith," at the Fourth Annual Abraham J. Malherbe Plenary, Christian Scholars Conference in Nashville, TN, on June 9, 2017. For a recording of Sterling's address, see https://ww2.lipscomb.edu/csc/lecture-and-plenary-speakers/2017-plenary-videos.

is. Scripture has all authority; tradition has none. That the situation is not so simple has sometimes been recognized, not least by pointing to positive references to tradition within the biblical text itself (e.g., 1 Cor. 11:2; 2 Thess. 2:15; 3:6). But often enough, any positive function for tradition has been regarded as entirely subsumed in the witness of the biblical text. Therefore, tradition as such is unnecessary and ineffective for proper biblical interpretation. Readers of Scripture are then entirely equipped for their task once they have Scripture alone as read through a proper interpretive method.

Unfortunately, after a century and a half, it is clear that the Restoration Movement has not been able to attain and maintain visible Christian unity by stressing uniformity in patternistic interpretive method. Instead,

> [e]ndless debates have ensued over which beliefs and practices are scriptural, which of those are necessary to salvation, and, in turn, who can be fellowshipped. Restoration, based on the Bible alone, pursued as a solution to the problem of division, has not fared much better with regard to unity than the confessional Presbyterianism from which the disenchanted founders departed.[2]

The expectation that a uniformity of interpretive method would result in Christian unity lies unrealized, and past decades suggest that future ones are not likely to fare much better. Clearly, the failure lies not with Scripture but with the kind of hermeneutic expectation that has been brought to Scripture.

In such a paradigm, the emphasis on Scripture's absolute authority surely is to be cherished. And the piety that animates a

[2] Keith D. Stanglin, "The Restoration Movement, the Habit of Schism, and a Proposal for Unity," *Christian Studies* 28 (2016): 12.

desire to faithfully obey this authority in all things is likewise to be desired and emulated. At the same time, it is largely the burden of this volume to suggest that—to adapt G. K. Chesterton's comment on Christianity in general—the Restoration plea has not been so much tried and found wanting as it has not yet been sufficiently heard and attempted.[3]

Instead of being actualized, the good and right impulse for the divine word to govern the church has been interpreted in ways proving inconsistent with that word. Originally, the impulse for Scripture alone to be the church's sole authority never meant to speak of Scripture's functioning in the absence of true and right Christian faith. Yet, Restorationism has often both identified its functioning Scripture as a pattern or model and isolated Scripture, reading the Bible as if in a vacuum, claiming to read and apply Scripture without the assistance of history or a tradition of faithful, receptive community.[4] As Keith Stanglin describes, the good and right Scripture-alone (*sola scriptura*) impulse became interpreted to mean that a much poorer "bare Scripture" (*nuda scriptura*) was what the church ought to have as a final authority.[5] Unfortunately, such a bare Scripture has ended up getting clothed with garments that have proven only too tattered and ill fitting.

---

[3]See G. K. Chesterton, *What's Wrong with the World* (New York: Dodd, Mead & Company, 1910), 48.

[4]To this day, restoration heirs remain familiar with the tension between a rejection of "tradition" in practicing biblical interpretation and an acknowledgment of the need for the church to be a contemporary community of interpretation. See M. Eugene Boring, *Disciples and the Bible: A History of Disciples Biblical Interpretation in North America* (St. Louis: Chalice Press, 1997).

[5]Keith D. Stanglin, *The Letter and Spirit of Biblical Interpretation: From the Early Church to Modern Practice* (Grand Rapids: Baker Academic, 2018), 130–32, 222. Stanglin employs the phrase from Brad S. Gregory, *The Unintended Reformation: How a Religious Revolution Secularized Society* (Cambridge, MA: Harvard University Press, 2012), 95.

Consequently, several essays in this volume critique the application of patternism when applied as a wholly sufficient and mechanically reliable interpretive method. But as the first two essays indicate, this challenge largely arises when patternism is reductively defined and understood. Such patternism falters because it needs to be informed by a richer, fuller reading of the biblical text.

Daniel B. Oden (Harding University) discusses this dynamic within the Old Testament. Oden observes how earlier Old Testament texts document and give rise to communal affirmations of Israel's beliefs about their God and their experience of him. Intending no anachronism, Oden terms these communal affirmations "creeds." He then traces how these creeds are rehearsed within and impact the formation of later Old Testament texts. In doing so, Oden shows how this traditional material is part and parcel to the Old Testament itself.

From the New Testament, J. David Stark (Kearley Graduate School of Theology) takes as a case study 1 Corinthians 15. At the beginning of that chapter, Paul explicitly cites traditional material that was formed early enough for him to receive it from others (vv. 1–5). Stark shows how the particular claim that the Messiah was raised according to the Scriptures (v. 4) provides Paul an interpretive starting point or basis for his scriptural interpretation in the balance of the chapter.

On the one hand, these essays show how tradition has become Scripture. On the other hand, both essays explore the ways in which this inscripturated tradition has determined how the biblical text defines what counts as proper engagement with itself. Consequently, these essays invite readers to a kind of patternism—but a patternism that is shaped by the often-overlooked ways in which the biblical text engages with itself. These essays demonstrate a biblical grounding for crystalizing certain core affirmations around which the people of God may cohere. And fidelity to the scriptural tradition requires that those who would read this tradition most fully should come under the sway of the core affirmations that the biblical text itself prioritizes.

The middle two essays especially address the Stone-Campbell heritage and its relationship to history. Keith D. Stanglin (Austin Graduate School of Theology) particularly focuses on the unity project Thomas Campbell articulates in his *Declaration and Address*. Acknowledging that there might be various appropriate goals for Christian work in different contexts, Stanglin argues that Campbell's main goal in his *Declaration and Address* was to foster Christian unity. Campbell had a clear program for how to achieve this unity. But what is often less appreciated is that Campbell also maintained an openness to other ways of faithfully achieving unity aside from (and perhaps more promising than) the one he proposed. Stanglin's essay thus shows how the Stone-Campbell tradition has—even at its earliest roots—a broader range of resources for fostering a faithful and unified Christian community. In particular, Stanglin recommends a reconsideration of the Apostles' Creed, of which Alexander Campbell explicitly approved, as a possible resource for fostering visible unity.

Stephen D. Lawson (Austin Graduate School of Theology) argues for a greater appreciation of the continuity of history between the time of the New Testament and the centuries in which the American Restoration Movement sprung into being. Lawson traces how some historical narratives within Stone-Campbell circles and other reform movements unhelpfully appeal to a cataclysmic fall narrative in which, after some pristine past period, all became malformed until whatever movement arrived on the scene to properly restore the primitive form. Lawson incisively warns of the dangers of this narrative, arguing that it invites the past to be remade in an image that is comfortable to the present and that thereby short circuits precisely the kind of reform efforts that appeal to this narrative.

The final two essays propose different practical turns for how guidance might be sought for biblical interpretation that will foster Christian unity. Scott Adair (Harding University) cites baptism as a prominent marker within Stone-Campbell circles of who does or does not share Christian identity. On this basis, Adair seeks to unpack the doctrinal and ethical content latent in baptismal practice. Because baptism admits people to Christian fellowship, Adair argues that Christians should prioritize the doctrinal and ethical content of the rite. In this way, baptism provides a locus for identifying what is central to Christian identity and what is not. The rite of baptism is many things. But in all of these, it is nothing less than a physical, visible enactment of core Christian commitments. Baptismal practice thereby invites readings of Scripture that focus on these central elements.

Lauren Smelser White (Lipscomb University) draws an analogy between maternal and hermeneutic discernment. Drawing on such noteworthy thinkers as Martin Luther, Karl Barth, and Hans Urs von Balthasar, White problematizes the notion that readers of Scripture can perform their task well at a distance. Instead, White urges, readers must risk getting themselves caught up in the biblical text's witness and finding themselves directly addressed by the text. This address is ultimately "Christomorphic," or one that shapes readers into the image of Christ. And for White, discerning a Christomorphic interpretation is fundamentally analogous to a mother's deeply embodied responsiveness in discerning how best to care for her child.

From these essays, there emerges an orientation to Scripture that emphasizes the need for hermeneutic engagement to be governed by a communally affirmed and deeply biblical "rule of faith," or "rule of truth," that can clarify precisely "the area in which the church hears the word of God."[6] The biblical text, subsequent Christian history, and current Christian practice all clearly show how properly and fully Christian biblical interpretation needs to be animated by a proper understanding, or "fore-conception," of what it seeks in the biblical text.[7] According to the early apologist Irenaeus of Lyons, biblical interpretation is problematic

> when a beautiful image of a king has been constructed by some skilful artist out of precious jewels, [and anyone] should then take this likeness of the man all to pieces, should re-arrange the gems, and so fit them together as to make them into the form of a dog or of a fox, and even that but poorly executed; and should then maintain and declare that this was the beautiful image of the king which the skilful artist constructed, pointing to the jewels which had been admirably fitted together by the first artist to form the image of the king, but have been with bad effect transferred by the latter one to the shape of a dog. . . . [On the other hand,] he . . . who retains unchangeable in his heart the rule of the truth which he received by means of baptism, will doubtless recognise the names, the expressions, and the parables taken from the Scriptures, but will by no means acknowledge the blasphemous use . . . of them. For, though he will acknowledge the gems, he will certainly not receive the fox instead of the likeness of the king. But when he has restored every one of the expressions quoted to its proper position, and has fitted it to the

[6] Brevard S. Childs, *Biblical Theology in Crisis* (Philadelphia: Westminster, 1970), 99.

[7] Cf. Hans-Georg Gadamer, *Truth and Method*, ed. and trans. Joel Weinsheimer and Donald G. Marshall, 2nd ed., Bloomsbury Revelations (London: Bloomsbury Academic, 2013), 305–6, 379, 443.

> body of the truth, he will lay bare, and prove to be without any foundation, the figment of these heretics.[8]

Not only does such a biblical "rule of truth" enable discernment of when biblical interpretation has gone awry, but it also enables readers to encounter Scripture precisely according to the image of the king whom they should properly find there.

With this volume's three pairs of essays, clearly a great many questions are left unresolved. For the present, the contributors have mainly tried to articulate a faithful starting point for biblical interpretation that might foster unity both within Stone-Campbell circles and beyond. In particular, there is a great need for the interpretive engagement with particular biblical texts along the lines suggested here. And we are hopeful that, in part, this volume will constitute an invitation to partnership in such readings and in refining the basic orientation proposed here.

In closing, we would like to thank each of the contributors for their efforts in making this volume as helpful as possible. We would also like to thank the several peers who, at various points, contributed helpful insights to assist in the refinement of this volume's individual essays. These include Fred Aquino (Abilene Christian University), Joshua Fleer (Oakland University), Mark Hamilton (Abilene Christian University), Ron Highfield (Pepperdine University), Noemí Palomares (Boston College), Floyd Parker (Faulkner University), Mark Powell (Harding School of Theology), Jared Saltz (Florida College), Mark Wiebe (Lubbock Christian University), and Kevin Youngblood (Harding University). We would also like to thank Jason Fikes and ACU Press for being such wonderful partners in bringing this volume to fruition. Finally, and most importantly, we would like to voice

[8]Irenaeus, "Against Heresies," §§1.8.1, 1.9.4, in *The Apostolic Fathers, Justin Martyr, Irenaeus*, ed. Alexander Roberts, James Donaldson, and A. Cleveland Coxe, Ante-Nicene Fathers 1 (Buffalo, NY: Christian Literature, 1885), 326, 330.

our inexpressible gratitude to our families (for Daniel: Helen, Jon, Dean, Zach, Ben, and Eliana; for David: Carrie, Ella, and Felicity) for their continued support throughout the various stages of this project's evolution. Without you, this volume would not have been possible.

1

Creedal Expressions and Their Development in the Hebrew Bible

Daniel B. Oden

The canon of Scripture has come to us through and within community—through the same community that also preserved tradition. As Keith Stanglin has reminded us, the interpretation of the Hebrew Scriptures was likewise first guided within the earliest Christian communities through baptismal formulas and a "common belief in the content of the apostolic proclamation," both of which appear in the New Testament of the later Christian community.[1] The purpose of this essay is to emphasize that within the Hebrew Scriptures, the creedal formulas that are spoken, recited, developed, and revised by the community were used as interpretative lenses in every stage of scriptural production and

[1]See Keith D. Stanglin, "The Restoration Movement, the Habit of Schism, and a Proposal for Unity," *Christian Studies* 28 (2016): 15.

I would like to thank Jared Saltz for reading and responding to an earlier version of this essay.

reception: forming, redacting, editing, receiving, and preserving the Scriptures.

Creedal Expressions in Hebrew Scripture

During the month of Sivan in synagogues around the world, congregations read the Torah portion *Sh'lach* (Num. 13:1–15:41). When they arrive in their reading at Numbers 14:18, they hear one of the first and greatest recitations in Scripture as Moses bravely recounts the Lord's proclamation of the divine character back to God, cooling God's anger against Israel for their refusal to enter the land. As Numbers 14:17 makes clear, Moses's recitation was an act of trust in God's revealed character, which the Lord had proclaimed to Moses when he appeared to him on Sinai following Israel's sin in worshiping the golden calf. That Numbers 14:17–18 may be considered a type of creedal statement is justified in part by the ubiquitous presence of its statement in varied forms throughout the Hebrew Bible.

Biblical writers incorporate creedal statements and their elements in narratives, rites, psalms, and prophetic oracles. For example, some direct parallels in phrases and distinct forms of the creedal statement are found among (1) Exodus 34:6–7 and Numbers 14:18; (2) Exodus 34:7 and Nahum 1:3; (3) Exodus 20:5 and Deuteronomy 5:9; (4) Psalms 86:15, 103:8, 145:8, Joel 2:13, and Jonah 4:2; and (5) Jeremiah 32:18 and Nehemiah 9:17. Many other biblical texts echo phrases from these primary forms or allude to specific elements of the creedal statement.[2] The similar formal characteristics and verbal expressions (elements) in multiple variants of the creedal statement, the fluidity of those elements, and their appearance and interpretative nuancing in different genres and settings throughout the Hebrew Scriptures (and perhaps

[2] For more examples, see Michael Widmer, "Moses, God, and the Dynamics of Intercessory Prayer" (PhD thesis, Durham University, 2003), 127. http://etheses.dur.ac.uk/3138/.

evidenced in an extrabiblical Hebrew inscription) are not only suggestive of a communal orality of the creed but demonstrative of the consistent transmission of it in multiple, related forms.

Whether the transmitting community is conjectured to be limited to smaller circles of literate elites, in royal, priestly, or priestly prophetic circles, or to have included a society of the mostly illiterate, who repeated or recited the creed in cultic or liturgical response, the function of a creedal statement is to guide (or challenge) readers in the proper interpretation of the surrounding text. Within the texts of Scripture, the creedal statement may affirm or defy biblical actors and speakers in interpreting a prophetic oracle; in the interpretation of an event or law; or, as in the case of Numbers 14:17–18, in interpreting the character of God. Therefore, in addition to differences in wording and variations in the phrasing of a given creedal form, there are often fragmentary, canonical "echoes" of the creed's discrete elements scattered throughout Scripture.

These fragmented echoes, however, particularly as witnessed in the Book of the Twelve (i.e., Hosea to Malachi, the minor prophets), are not simply isolated forms or memories but pieces of a puzzle that join together the different minor prophets, designing a holistic message out of their diverse historical settings, theological emphases, and rhetorical strategies. That creeds are also "recitals" stems from another aspect of such statements that differentiates creedal expressions from other summaries of dogma: the statements to which we appeal in the Hebrew Bible are creedal in that they are written as if spoken. Creeds are spoken in a register of profession or recital. The examples discussed in this essay originate in divine speech but become the core for prophetic intercessory prayer (Num. 14:18) and community recital (Deut. 5:1–6:25).

Further, it is clear that the "biblical reader" is not primarily an individual but a community, whether a prophetic house, priestly scribes, or a royal chancellery (in the Scriptures' early formative periods); or the synagogue, a sectarian community, the temple priesthood; or the Jesus movement (during the Scriptures' continued development into these later receptive periods).[3] As Robert W. Jenson has observed, "The community positioned to perceive what a scriptural text is truly up to is the church, and the creed is the set of instructions for discerning this agenda."[4]

Creedal Recital in the Hebrew Scriptures

Mark Boda's recent work *The Heartbeat of Old Testament Theology* informs these observations, as he ties together a unified theology from the diverse tapestry of the canon of the Hebrew Bible by selectively identifying "core expressions of God that appear throughout the [Old Testament] canon."[5] Boda hears three rhythms of Old Testament theology—the first being a narrative rhythm that echoes the emphasis on salvation history (*Heilsgeschichte*) in the works of Geerhardus Vos, Gerhard von Rad, and G. E. Wright. As Wright stated, "Biblical Theology is the *confessional recital of the redemptive acts of God*."[6] Von Rad emphasized short historical creeds (*kleine geschichtliche Credo*), which are typically communally

---

[3]For works that examine the scribal practices and social institutions that shaped literacy and texts in the ancient Levant, ancient Israel, Judah, and post-exilic Yahud, see David M. Carr, *Writing on the Tablet of the Heart: Origins of Scripture and Literature* (Oxford: Oxford University Press, 2008), 111–286; Seth L. Sanders, *The Invention of Hebrew* (Urbana: University of Illinois Press, 2009), 76–172; William M. Schniedewind, *How the Bible Became a Book* (Cambridge: Cambridge University Press, 2005), 48–194; and Karel van der Toorn, *Scribal Culture and the Making of the Hebrew Bible* (Cambridge, MA: Harvard University Press, 2007), 109–265.

[4]Robert W. Jenson, *Canon and Creed*, Interpretation (Louisville: Westminster John Knox Press, 2010), 81. Early restorationists, to their credit, assumed this principle in their then contemporary practice. See M. Eugene Boring, *Disciples and the Bible: A History of Disciples Biblical Interpretation in North America* (St. Louis: Chalice Press, 1997), 25–26.

[5]Mark Boda, *The Heartbeat of Old Testament Theology: Three Creedal Expressions* (Grand Rapids: Baker Academic, 2017), 7.

[6]Boda, *Heartbeat of Old Testament Theology*, 10n3.

recited summaries of God's redemptive acts in Scripture (Deut. 6:21–23; 26:5–9) but can also be expressed as divine revelation, such as is found in Joshua 24:2–13.[7] Boda performs a selective analysis of the texts most commonly identified as confessional recitals of God's acts and identifies several actions that recur throughout these texts.[8] He explains that the "core actions" of the Old Testament's narrative creedal expressions are the Exodus and Conquest narratives. Actions involving the ancestors, wilderness traditions, life in the land, destruction, and exile "extend" God's core narrative actions in Israel's memory. Exodus 32–34 and Numbers 13–14 appear in the second theological rhythm Boda monitors: a rhythm he designates as "the character rhythm."[9] Here, Brevard Childs detected the pulse of God's character as creedal confession, in which the "frequent use" of Exodus 34:6–7 throughout the Hebrew Bible "is an eloquent testimony to the centrality of this understanding of God's person."[10]

> The LORD passed before him, and pronounced: "The LORD, the LORD, a God merciful and gracious, slow to anger, and abundant in faithful love and faithfulness, keeping faithful love to the thousandth generation, forgiving iniquity and transgression and sin, but by no means clearing the guilty: visiting the iniquity of the parents on children and children's children, unto the third and the fourth generation."[11]

---

[7] Boda, *Heartbeat of Old Testament Theology*, 12–13.

[8] Exod. 15:1–19; Deut. 6:21–23, 26:5–9, 29:2–9, 32:1–47; Josh. 24:2–13; Judg. 2:1–3, 6:8–10, 11:16–24; 1 Sam. 12:8; Ps. 78:1–72, 105:1–45, 106:1–48, 135:1–21; Neh. 9:6–31; Jer. 2:6–7, 32:17–23; Ezek. 20:5–29.

[9] Boda, *Heartbeat of Old Testament Theology*, 27–51.

[10] Boda, *Heartbeat of Old Testament Theology*, 28, citing Brevard S. Childs, *The Book of Exodus: A Critical, Theological Commentary*, Old Testament Library (Philadelphia: Westminster John Knox Press, 1974), 612.

[11] Unless otherwise indicated, Scripture translations are the author's.

God's steadfast love (*ḥesed*) and severe justice (expressed above in the phrase *pōqēd ʿăwōn ʾābôt,* "visiting the iniquity of the parents") are the core characteristics of this creedal expression. The final rhythm that Boda detects he calls the "relational rhythm," an alliterative appellation for covenantal theology. The core elements of relational creeds center on God and Father. Texts in which Boda hears this third creedal expression include Genesis 17:7–8; Exodus 6:7; Leviticus 11:45, 22:33, 25:38, 26:12; Numbers 15:41; Deuteronomy 29:12 (Eng. v. 13); 2 Samuel 7:14; Jeremiah 31:33; Psalms 89:27–28; and 1 Chronicles 17:13; 22:10.[12]

Boda's book is an excellent contribution to Old Testament theology that creatively integrates all three rhythms or expressions throughout the entirety of the Protestant Christian canon, including their influence on the New Testament and the present Christian community. For the purpose of this essay, Boda's identification and analysis of repeated, summarizing, confessional biblical creeds supports the idea that biblical creedal statements serve as exegetical lenses through which the developing prophetic oracles and narrative traditions were read by the community.

Returning to Exodus 32–34 and Numbers 13–14 illustrates Boda's observed, ubiquitous characteristic of the Hebrew Scriptures: contextualized creedal expressions serve as theological confessions and unifying statements for the community and a means by which the community is taught to read the Torah and interpret prophecy.[13]

---

[12] Boda, *Heartbeat of Old Testament Theology*, 54–55.

[13] In relation to the two creedal texts discussed in this essay, see (1) Isa. 11:16, Hosea 2:17 (Eng. v. 15), and Mic. 6:4 in relation to Exod. 20:1 and 32:6; and (2) Mic. 7:18, Ezek. 44:10–12, and Nah. 1:3 in relation to Exod. 34:6–7 and Num. 14:17–18. The influence of these creedal summaries as hermeneutics that frame the community's theological interpretation of the Torah and prophecy is further suggested by Ezekiel's protracted rebuttal of the community's interpretation of the principle of divine collective punishment in Ezek. 18.

Numbers 14:17–18, Exodus 34:6–7, and Their Parallels

The close literary relationship between Numbers 14:18 and Exodus 34:6–7, while generating no overwhelming scholarly consensus regarding each passage's independent origin and development, is nonetheless a commonly accepted tenet of biblical studies.[14] Comparison of the two texts reveals their general agreement, the distinct elements shared by both when compared to other biblical examples of the creed, as well as their differences.[15]

> וַיַּעֲבֹר יְהוָה עַל־פָּנָיו וַיִּקְרָא יְהוָה יְהוָה אֵל רַחוּם וְחַנּוּן אֶרֶךְ אַפַּיִם וְרַב־חֶסֶד
> וֶאֱמֶת נֹצֵר חֶסֶד לָאֲלָפִים נֹשֵׂא עָוֺן וָפֶשַׁע וְחַטָּאָה וְנַקֵּה לֹא יְנַקֶּה פֹּקֵד עֲוֺן
> אָבוֹת עַל־בָּנִים וְעַל־בְּנֵי בָנִים עַל־שִׁלֵּשִׁים וְעַל־רִבֵּעִים

> The LORD passed before him, and pronounced: "The LORD, **the LORD**, a God merciful and gracious, **slow to anger, and abundant in faithful love** and faithfulness, keeping faithful love to the thousandth generation, **forgiving iniquity and transgression** and sin, **but by no means clearing the guilty: visiting the iniquity of the parents on children** and children's children, **unto the third and the fourth generation**." (Exod. 34:6–7)

---

[14] See J. P. Bosnan, "The Paradoxical Presence of Exodus 34:6–7 in the Book of the Twelve," *Scriptura* 87 (2004): 233–43; Mark A. O'Brien, "The Dynamics of the Golden Calf Story (Exodus 32–34)," *Australian Biblical Review* 60 (2012): 18–31; H. Spieckermann, "Barmherzig und gnädig ist der Herr . . .," *Zeitschrift für die alttestamentliche Wissenschaft* 102 (1990): 1–18; Michael Widmer, *Moses, God, and the Dynamics of Intercessory Prayer: A Study of Exodus 32–34 and Numbers 13–14*, Forschungen zum Alten Testament 2/8 (Stuttgart: Mohr Siebeck, 2004).

[15] In the comparison of examples of this creedal statement in the Hebrew Bible undertaken in this essay, I partially have relied on Abba Bendavid, *Parallels in the Bible* (Jerusalem: Carta, 1965), 182–83 (in Hebrew). The text of the Hebrew Bible used throughout this essay is the Accordance Bible electronic edition (BHS-T) of Karl Elliger and Wilhelm Rudolph, eds., *Biblia Hebraica Stuttgartensia,* 5th rev. ed. prepared by Adrian Schenker (Stuttgart: Deutsche Bibelgesellschaft, 1997).

וְעַתָּה יִגְדַּל־נָא כֹּחַ אֲדֹנָי כַּאֲשֶׁר דִּבַּרְתָּ לֵאמֹר יְהוָה אֶרֶךְ אַפַּיִם וְרַב־חֶסֶד נֹשֵׂא
עָוֹן וָפָשַׁע וְנַקֵּה לֹא יְנַקֶּה פֹּקֵד עֲוֹן אָבוֹת עַל־בָּנִים עַל־שִׁלֵּשִׁים וְעַל־רִבֵּעִים

> And now, may the power of the Lord be great—as when you previously spoke, saying, "**The Lord—slow to anger, and abundant in faithful love, forgiving iniquity and transgression, but by no means clearing the guilty: visiting the iniquity of parents on children, unto the third and the fourth** (**generation**)." (Num. 14:17–18)

The recitation of the creedal statements of Exodus 34:6–7 and Numbers 14:17–18 occurs at significant moments in the historical narratives of Israel and in the redaction of the Pentateuch. As such, this foundational belief statement describing the character of God serves as both an interpretative foundation and a foil for the community of exiles, its prophets, and its scribes. Its presence and function within the Book of the Twelve further solidifies the formative nature of this scriptural creed.[16] The creed's phrases may serve as a framework for the oracles of doom (Nah. 1:3) or laments (Jer. 15:15; Ps. 86:15–16a), as an exegetical lens through which to interpret prophetic oracles and books (Jon. 4:2), or as an inspiration for the "responsive-creeds" of Judah (Ezek. 18; Jer. 16). (In the following discussion, however, I do not presume to have exhaustively identified allusions within the Hebrew Scriptures to the character creedal statements of Exodus 34:6–7 and Numbers 14:17–18.)

Exodus 34:6–7 presents the most expansive version of the creedal statement in Scripture, including several phrases found in the prophetic and poetic forms of the creedal statement that are not present in Numbers 14:17–18. These phrases include אֵל רַחוּם וְחַנּוּן

[16] J. P. Bosnan, "The Paradoxical Presence," 238–42, notes the influence of Exod. 34:6–7 in the Book of the Twelve in Hosea 1:6, Joel 2:13, Jonah 4:2, Mic. 7:18–20, and Nah. 1:3a.

("a God merciful and gracious"), variations of which are found in Psalms 86:15, 103:8, 145:8; Joel 2:13; Jonah 4:2; and Nehemiah 9:17; וֶאֱמֶת ("and faithfulness"), shared only with Psalm 86:15; נֹצֵר חֶסֶד לָאֲלָפִים ("keeping faithful love to the thousandth generation"), shared with Exodus 20:5, Deuteronomy 5:10, and Jeremiah 32:18 (which render the phrase עֹשֶׂה חֶסֶד לַאֲלָפִים—literally "doing faithful love to thousands"); and וְעַל־בְּנֵי בָנִים ("and the children's children"), a phrase unique to the version of the statement in Exodus 34:7.

The entirety of the statement in Numbers 14:17–18 is found within that of Exodus 34:6–7. Of the phrases that appear in both texts, אֶרֶךְ אַפַּיִם ("slow to anger") always appears preceded by the divine name or other divine titulary (such as אֵל רַחוּם וְחַנּוּן, "God merciful and gracious") in creedal contexts (Jon. 4:2; Nah. 1:3; Ps. 86:15, 103:8, 145:8; Neh. 9:17). In texts that likely allude to the creedal statement, such as Isaiah 48:9 and Jeremiah 15:15, the phrase אֶרֶךְ אַפַּיִם ("slow to anger") similarly describes or assumes the divine character expressed in the creed. Only in the frequent use of the phrase אֶרֶךְ אַפַּיִם ("slow to anger") in Proverbs is the phrase not preceded by a divine titulary (Prov. 14:29, 15:18, 16:32, 19:11, 25:15). However, it is likely that these proverbs should be understood in light of the ubiquitous creedal context of the phrase—one who is "slow to anger" shares the divine character—see especially Prov. 14:29, where the phrase "slow to anger" is followed not by רַב־חֶסֶד ("abundant in faithful love") but by רַב־תְּבוּנָה ("abundant in understanding"). The phrase נֹשֵׂא עָוֹן וָפֶשַׁע ("forgiving iniquity and transgression") occurs only in the creedal statements of Exodus 34:6–7 and Numbers 14:17–18, while וְנַקֵּה לֹא יְנַקֶּה ("but by no means clearing the guilty") occurs elsewhere only in the creedal statement of Nahum 1:3, though a variation of this phrase appears in the divine speech of Jeremiah 30:11 and 46:28 (a repeated oracle against the nations). Finally, the last phrase, פֹּקֵד עֲוֹן אָבוֹת עַל־בָּנִים וְעַל־בְּנֵי בָנִים עַל־שִׁלֵּשִׁים וְעַל־רִבֵּעִים ("visiting the iniquity of parents on children unto the third and the fourth") appears elsewhere only in

Exodus 20:5 and Deuteronomy 5:9. One may see allusions to the phrase פֹּקֵד עֲוֹן ("visiting the iniquity of . . ."), employing finite and infinitive forms of the root פקד ("to visit") paired with the noun עֲוֹן ("iniquity of") in Leviticus 18:25, Isaiah 26:21, and Lamentations 4:22. All of these allusions either describe divine action or are written as divine speech.

In addition to the biblical texts presented here, inscriptional evidence from Judah suggests that some of the elements included in the biblical creedal statement of Exodus 34:6–7 and echoed throughout the Hebrew Bible were independently "recited" in ancient Judah. An inscription discovered in a burial cave near Khirbet Beit Lei (*BLei* 6), dated by some to the eighth to sixth centuries BCE, but by others to the Hellenistic era, may share three elements of the creedal phrasing of Exodus 34:6–7: פקד יה אל חנן נקה יה יהוה ("Attend! O gracious God! Acquit! O YHWH!").[17] Alice Mandell and Jeremy Smoak have argued sensibly for greater attention to the funerary context of the inscription. However, their focus on the function of the inscriptions in its original place (in situ) may risk deadening the voice of the text, as if there was no

[17]The reading is that in F. W. Dobbs-Allsopp, J. J. M. Roberts, C. J. Seow, R. E. Whitaker, eds., *Hebrew Inscriptions: Texts from the Biblical Period of the Monarchy with Concordance* (New Haven, CT: Yale University Press, 2005), 130–31. For alternative readings of the inscription, see A. Lemaire, "*Prières en temps de crise: Les inscriptions de Khirbet Beit Lei*," *Revue Biblique* 84, no. 4 (1976): 558–68. The word *yh*, repeated in the inscription, is understood here as a vocative particle rather than an alternate form of the divine name. See Dobbs-Allsopp et al., *Hebrew Inscriptions*, 131, and Nadav Naʿaman, "The Israelite-Judahite Struggle for the Patrimony of Ancient Israel," *Biblica* 91, no. 1 (2010): 1–23. Alternatively, if one understands *yh* to be a form of the divine name, the repetition of the divine name, *yh yhwh*, could be akin to that in Exod. 34:6–7. See P. D. Miller, "Psalms and Inscriptions," *Supplements to Vetus Testamentum* 32 (1981): 311–32. For the view that the material context suggests a Hellenistic era date, see A. Mandell and J. D. Smoak, "Reconsidering the Function of Tomb Inscriptions in Iron Age Judah: Khirbet Beit Lei as a Test Case," *Journal of Ancient Near Eastern Religions* 16, no. 2 (2016): 197.

connection between the funerary inscription and likely living recitations of the formula outside the cave.[18]

Exodus 34:6–7, Numbers 14:17–18, and Their Narrative Contexts

Within the golden-calf narrative of the failure of Israel at Sinai (Exod. 32–34) and the story of the failure of the people to enter the land (Num. 13–14), the recitation of God's character is an integral element of each narrative's plot and structure. Moreover, the two narratives, in which the creedal statement and its recitation are embedded, share other parallel structural elements and techniques of narrative crafting. Direct verbal correspondences between the two narratives are few, limited mainly to the recitation of the creedal statement. Yet the relative lack of shared, verbatim expressions brings common structural plot elements and narrative crafting to the fore.

In each narrative, after an episode of the people's rebellion, and after a period of waiting for forty days (Exod. 32:1–8; cf. Exod. 24:18 and Num. 13:25–14:10), the Lord appears, declaring he will destroy the nation and create a new nation through Moses alone (Exod. 32:9–10; Num. 14:11–12). Moses intercedes on behalf of the people in both narratives, reminding the Lord that the Egyptians will hear of the people's destruction and ridicule the Lord or the Lord's people (Exod. 32:11–12; Num. 14:13–16). In Exodus 32:13–14, Moses reminds the Lord of the promises he swore to the patriarchs, causing the Lord "to relent from the disaster he spoke of doing to his people." Moses repeats the divine recital of the Lord's character creed (Exod. 34:6–7) in Numbers 14:10, and the Lord pardons the iniquity of the people on the basis of Moses's recitation of the creed (Num. 14:20): סָלַחְתִּי כִּדְבָרֶךָ ("I have pardoned—according to

[18] For a rebuttal of previous scholarship on both the dating of the inscriptions at Khirbet Beit Lei and an affirmation of the contextual relationship of the inscriptions to their material, funerary setting, see Mandell and Smoak, "Reconsidering the Function of Tomb Inscriptions," 192–245.

your word"). Notwithstanding the pardon of Numbers 14:20, both narratives then move to describe an immediate punishment by plague against a portion of the people (Exod. 32:35; Num. 14:37).

The primary difference in the use of the creedal statement in the two narratives is that in Numbers 13–14, the recited creed becomes the basis for Moses's appeal for divine pardon, which is granted: "I have pardoned, *according to your word*." Nonetheless, pardon is not granted to עֵדָה הָרָעָה הַזֹּאת ("this evil generation"; Num. 14:21–23, 26–35), excepting the households of Joshua and Caleb. Further, all of the children of the "evil" Exodus generation suffer along with their parents during the forty-year duration of divine punishment (Num. 14:33).

In Exodus 32–34, Moses's plea for divine pardon is answered by the Lord with a plague as punishment, though limited to the individuals who sinned against the Lord (Exod. 32:22). Moreover, the Lord never explicitly pardons the people in the matter of the golden calf, unless one infers pardon from the Lord's relenting in bringing disaster to the entire community. Rather, the divinely proclaimed creed of Exodus 34:6–7 becomes the basis for a new iteration of the Sinai covenant (see Exod. 34:1–35:29).

Interestingly then, Exodus 32–34 and Numbers 13–14 know not only the creed as recited within their own narratives, ending in transgenerational punishment, but both narratives evoke the "revised" creed of Deuteronomy 7:9–10: "You know that the LORD your God, he is God; the trusted God who keeps covenant and faithful love for those who love him, those keeping his commandments, to a thousand generations—yet repaying to his face the one who hates him, by destroying him. He will not delay with one who hates him. He will repay him to his face." Those who are guilty die, and their children endure a visitation of divine recompense, limited to the lifetime of the evil generation.

Anticreedal Recital in the Hebrew Scriptures. A variation of the "character" creedal statements of Exodus 34:6–7 and Numbers 14:17–18 appears in the second commandment according to the Jewish order (Exod. 20:5–6; Deut. 5:9–10). Yet the Ten Commandments or "Ten Words" begin with a distinctive creedal expression, a "salvation-history" creedal statement that, like the "character creed" of Exodus 34:5–7, is found throughout the Hebrew Scriptures: "I am the LORD your God who brought you out of the land of Egypt, out of the house of slavery." The first "word" (Exod. 20:2; Deut. 5:6) is a declaration, an oration, and more like a creed than a commandment. In an ironic twist, this salvation-history creed becomes a "negative creed" or heterodox creed when Aaron recites it almost verbatim in Exodus 32:6, in reference to deities enthroned upon (or represented by) the golden calf crafted out of the people's earrings: "These are your gods who brought you out of [or, up from] the land of Egypt." In fact, this creed nowhere appears in an orthodox form in Exodus 32, whether in v. 1, where the people recite the anticreed in their derisive comments about Moses, or when their words are paraphrased by Aaron in v. 23:

> When the people saw that Moses delayed to come down from the mountain, the people gathered around Aaron, and said to him, "Come, make gods for us, who shall go before us; as for this Moses, the man who brought us up out of the land of Egypt, we do not know what has become of him." (NRSV)

One must wait for the second giving of the law to hear again the orthodox version of this short creed in Deuteronomy 20:1: "Whenever you set out to battle against your enemies, and you see horse and chariot, a people, many more than your own, you shall not fear them; for the LORD your God is with you, who brought you up from the land of Egypt." Deuteronomy 20:1 seems more evocative of the Numbers 13–14 spies narrative than either the decalogue setting of Exodus 20 and Deuteronomy 5 or the golden-calf narrative of Exodus 32–34.

Elaborate, intentional narrative crafting and shared theological expressions have shaped and informed the "calf/calves" narratives of Exodus 32–34 and 1 Kings 12–14.[19] Among the elements indicating a close textual relationship between 1 Kings 12–14 and Exodus 32–34, one finds a shared creedal expression (more accurately, an anticreed). A foundational section of the so-called Deuteronomistic history, 1 Kings 12:28 shares with Exodus 32–34 the famous negative creed of Aaron in Exodus 32:4. Jeroboam made two calves of gold, one of which he set in Bethel and the other in Dan, to discourage Israel from returning to the temple in Jerusalem. When he first presented the calves to the people, Jeroboam recited Aaron's anticreed: "These are your gods, O Israel, which brought you up from the land of Egypt."

Regardless of the original direction of compositional influence, one sees in these two accounts a reflective process of editing by a community (or communities) committed to remembering and interpreting their past and present through the recital of such creedal expressions. Thus a common theological identity and unity are created, perpetuated, and reinforced, while competing theological expressions are rejected. The distortion of the creed in Exodus 32:4 (reported in 32:8) denies the orthodox monotheism that the reciting community knows is demanded of them. In form and, acutely, in pronunciation, the heterodox creed is almost correct. The minimal (but profound) variation occurs in

---

[19] On the relationship between Exod. 32–34 and 1 Kings 12–14, see M. Aberbach and L. Smolar, "Aaron, Jeroboam and the Golden Calves," *Journal of Biblical Literature* 86, no. 2 (1967): 129–40; S. Lasine, "Reading Jeroboam's Intentions: Intertextuality, Rhetoric and History in 1 Kings 12," in *Reading Between Texts: Intertextuality and the Hebrew Bible*, ed. D. N. Fewell (Louisville: Westminster John Knox Press, 1992), 133–52; M. Leuchter, "Jeroboam the Ephratite," *Journal of Biblical Literature* 125, no. 1 (2006): 51–72.

the plural verbs of the dependent adjectival noun clause: "These are your gods, O Israel, who brought you up from the land of Egypt," rather than "For the LORD your God is with you, who brought you up from the land of Egypt." Thus, hearing Jeroboam recite the heterodox creed of Exodus 32:4 in 1 Kings 12:28 in reference to the calves he erected at Dan and Bethel informs the reading community that the sin of Jeroboam is not simply an illegitimate cultic and political appropriation of the Exodus-salvation narrative (*Heilsgeschichte*) but also a denial of the divine nature and sovereignty of the God of Israel. Perhaps more importantly, recital of the anticreed, though initially drawing the community's ear to Exodus 32:4, invites the community to return to Exodus 20 (Deut. 5). The corrective to Aaron's and Jeroboam's heterodox confession, Exodus 20:1 (Deut. 5:6), draws the community deeper into the recitation of the divine character as it is revealed in the Ten Words, Exodus 20:4–6 (Deut. 5:9–10):

> You shall not make for yourself an idol, whether in the form of anything that is in heaven above, or that is on the earth beneath, or that is in the water under the earth. You shall not bow down to them or worship them; for I the LORD your God am a jealous God, punishing children for the iniquity of parents, to the third and the fourth generation of those who reject me, but showing steadfast love to the thousandth generation of those who love me and keep my commandments. (NRSV)

The historian of Kings connects for his readers Jeroboam's sin to Aaron's and Israel's sin at Sinai. In so doing, the editor of Kings also reconnects the reader to the orthodox creed in the divinely written tablets from Sinai. Jeroboam's anticreed, coupled with his calves and rival altars, reminds readers of Kings about the character of the saving God who brought Israel out of Egypt, whose stern justice results in transgenerational punishment, albeit for transgenerational sin. (That Kings and Deuteronomy are here reciting a developed creed, one addressing not only transgenerational punishment but also transgenerational sin, will be addressed later.) Nadab's perpetuation of his father's cultic transgressions is explicit (1 Kings 15:26, 30), insinuating the character creed as stated in Exodus 20:4–6 (Deut. 5:9–10). Jeroboam's dynasty will be limited to one descendant, Nadab, whose reign will be cut short by Baasha, son of Ahijah (1 Kings 15:27).[20] Correspondingly, 1 Kings 15 begins with the application of the creedal statement's principle of transgenerational mercy and reward. For the sake of David, his righteousness (הַיָּשָׁר) was extended to the third generation of his dynasty (1 Kings 15:1–5). While Jeroboam's heir Nadab is punished in fulfillment of Jehu's prophecy, the sins of Rehoboam's heir Abijam are covered for David's sake, even though Abijam continued in Rehoboam's sins. The content and structure of 1 Kings 15 intentionally reflect elements of the statements in Exodus 20:1–4 (Deut. 5:6–10), which articulate and interpret these foundational creedal confessions of the Hebrew Bible.

On one hand, these creedal and anticreedal expressions appear in narratives that repeat the story of God's redemption of Israel in the powerful acts he performed in bringing about the nation's exodus from Egypt. On the other hand, the repetition and echoing of these key creedal texts in different narrative traditions suggest that the texts are not merely passengers in the biblical narrative, but are used intentionally to shape the present form and content of the narratives, accounting for much of the intertextuality that scholars see in Exodus 32–24, Numbers 13–14, and 1 Kings 12–14. That is, regardless of the antiquity of the creedal expression themselves, their employment in these

[20] I have benefitted here from B. Levenson, "The Human Voice in Revelation: The Problem of Authority in Biblical Law," in *Innovations in Religious Traditions: Essays in the Interpretation of Religious Change*, ed. M. A. Williams, C. Cox, and M. S. Jaffee (Berlin: Mouton de Gruyter, 1992), 48.

complex narratives, built from putative pluriform traditions, unifies the accounts. The confessional statement serves as a kind of "canonical tissue" that connects and unifies originally discreet traditions, all of which cohere around the activity of the same deity whose character is articulated in the variations of the creedal statement.[21] One surmises that a key purpose of these intentional scribal and theological practices was that of forming and maintaining a harmonious, healthy, and unified community, even one far removed in time and place from the events described in the narratives.

The narrative of Numbers 13–14 also retells the story of God's redemption of Israel from Egypt, with close associations to Exodus 32–34, but here the setting of the orthodox creed of Numbers 14:18 integrates all three of Boda's expressions. God's anger rises when it is clear that the salvation-history creed of redemption in the Exodus narrative is lost on the Israelites in the wilderness, whose derision of Moses has turned to derision of the Lord: "And the LORD said to Moses, 'How long will this people despise me? And how long will they not trust in me, in all the signs that I have done among them?'" (Num. 14:11). In Moses's intercession for the people, he recites what Boda calls a "relational" expression by appealing to God's presence among his people (an indication of his steadfast love). God's presence is expressed in God's self-revelation through core covenantal promises, which are ultimately upheld by God's righteousness, not Israel's obedience. Moses does not ask God to deny God's own holiness or justice. Therefore, the creedal statement is not simply a recital of a principle, but becomes an appeal to a living being, whose aseity may be expressed in both punishment and in the provision of extraordinary forgiveness, so that divine ability is not misconstrued among the nations:

[21] I am indebted to Kevin Youngblood for this observation in his helpful review of this essay, which incorporates several of his suggestions.

> But Moses said to the LORD, "Then the Egyptians will hear of it, for in your might you brought up this people from among them, and they will tell the inhabitants of this land. They have heard that you, O LORD, are in the midst of this people; for you, O LORD, are seen face to face, and your cloud stands over them and you go in front of them, in a pillar of cloud by day and in a pillar of fire by night. Now if you kill this people all at one time, then the nations who have heard about you will say, 'It is because the LORD was not able to bring this people into the land he swore to give them that he has slaughtered them in the wilderness.' . . . Forgive the iniquity of this people according to the greatness of your steadfast love, just as you have pardoned this people, from Egypt even until now." (Num. 14:13–16, 19 NRSV)

Here, the creedal formula appears in a context where Moses is interceding to prevent Israel's destruction, recalling the earlier (at least canonically) case of Moses's successful intercession in Exodus 32–34. The creed in this context serves as a canonical thread, connecting the rebellion episodes in order to encourage the community to read and interpret them in reference to each other.

Scripture as Exegetical Commentary

Among the most influential works of biblical interpretation published in the twentieth century, one may include Michael Fishbane's *Biblical Interpretation in Ancient Israel*, in which Fishbane explored the development of biblical traditions, describing the processes of their transmission (*traditio*), and especially focused on the practice of exegesis *within* the Hebrew Bible.[22] According to Fishbane, biblical scholarship of the previous two centuries largely raised

[22] Fishbane, *Biblical Interpretation in Ancient Israel*, 3.

questions about the diachronic development of biblical texts from prebiblical sources and traditions. Tradition history, rooted in the historical-philological method, supposes that the content of any particular tradition, a *traditum* (whether a legal document, cultic rule, narrative motif, or poetic fragment), was preserved and received into biblical texts through *traditio*, a "long and varied process of transmission."[23] The tradition-history approach to Scripture, raising questions about its earlier literary and oral stages, remains a valuable discipline, though its results are often speculative and tenuous, as sometimes observed even by its most influential practitioners.[24]

Less speculative is the application of the methods of tradition history for the study of the postbiblical exegesis seen in the New Testament and other Second Temple Jewish literature. Here, the texts of the Hebrew Bible and other Jewish texts, as *traditum*, appear in the process of their transmission into these later literatures (*traditio*), interpreted with fresh eyes by the newly formed communities. By means of their reinterpretation, a new *traditum* emerges. Or, more specifically, an old *traditum*, preserved on account of its authority for the later community (*traditio*), is reinterpreted by its later readers, who exert their own (subordinating) authority in their exegesis. The authority of the old *traditum* is observed, but the content and context of the old *traditum* are redefined, conceivably even displacing the old *traditum*, in the process of interpretation. Under the authority of the old *traditum*, a new *traditum* is established, through the process of interpretation (*traditio*). Fishbane's purpose is to demonstrate that one does not have to wait until the postbiblical period of Second Temple interpretation to see exegetical processes: exegesis is already occurring within the biblical text itself. To prove

[23] Fishbane, *Biblical Interpretation in Ancient Israel*, 6.

[24] See Fishbane's discussion of Martin Noth. Fishbane, *Biblical Interpretation in Ancient Israel*, 8.

this concept, Fishbane locates within the biblical text an example in which an established legal *datum* (*traditum*) is exegeted by an authoritative teacher who incorporates into the general *traditum* a specific interpretation in the process of interpretation (*traditio*) and thereby teaches the *traditum* to a new generation. Fishbane refers us to Numbers 15:22–31, in which a third party (not the Lord or Moses, the sources of the *traditum*), the narrator, as a preacher of Torah "teaches and interprets the divine law."[25] The relevant portion of this text follows:

> But if you unintentionally fail to observe all these commandments that the Lord has spoken to Moses—everything that the Lord has commanded you by Moses, from the day the Lord gave commandment and thereafter, throughout your generations—then if it was done unintentionally without the knowledge of the congregation, the whole congregation shall offer one young bull for a burnt offering. . . . All the congregation of the Israelites shall be forgiven, as well as the aliens residing among them, because the whole people was involved in the error. (Num. 15:22–24a, 26 NRSV)

Fishbane draws the conclusion: "That this *traditio* is now incorporated into the established legal *traditum* not only authorizes and legitimates the new teaching for all time, but indicates that the *traditio* of the exegetical teacher was formally and functionally subordinate to the divine revelation. And, what is more, it means that the teacher does not stand forth alone, on his own authority."[26]

To state it simply, Fishbane argues that a straightforward reading of Numbers 15:22–31 indicates that this explanatory pericope does not belong to an original transmission of revelation from the Lord to Moses (*datum* or *traditum*). Rather, this portion of

[25] Fishbane, *Biblical Interpretation in Ancient Israel*, 260.
[26] Fishbane, *Biblical Interpretation in Ancient Israel*, 261.

Numbers is *via traditio* from a later teacher, in which the teacher explains and applies the earlier legislation given to Moses to the teacher's (later) community. Fishbane describes this phenomenon that appears in the Hebrew Bible as a revelation-tradition dialectic, in which it is noteworthy that human exegetical authority (namely, any exegetical activity) is observable in biblical legal and historiographical contexts, even into the post-exilic period.[27]

Moving from more explicitly marked examples of scribal exegesis, expressed by means of technical terms used in the Masoretic text, to the observed transmission of Hebrew Bible textual variants (differences between Qumran, Septuagint, and Masoretic manuscripts) and parallel texts (such as revision in Chronicles and Samuel/Kings), to scribal editorial glosses, pious revisions, and theological explanations, Fishbane proceeds to describe inner-biblical exegesis in three categories: legal (halakhic explanation and revision), aggadic (theological and narrative explanation), and mantological (prophetic/oracular/vision explanation).

The implications of these principles of *traditum* and *traditio*, if accurate descriptions of some aspects in the development of the canonical Hebrew Scriptures, are profound. Fishbane is not proposing that the exegetical activity of revelation (*traditio*) belongs only to the periods subsequent to the formation of the canon; on the contrary, commentary on revelation (*traditum*) first appears prior to the canon's final fixed form.[28]

The Nexus of Narrative, Creed, and Commentary: Developments throughout Scripture

The creedal modifications and development that primarily concern one here are the explanations and clarifications appearing throughout the Hebrew Bible in reference to the closing phrases

[27] Fishbane, *Biblical Interpretation in Ancient Israel*, 16.

[28] See Levenson and the concepts of biblical "lemmatic citation" and "lemmatic exegesis" in "The Human Voice in Revelation," 37–38.

of the character creed, "visiting the iniquity of the ancestors on the children, and on the grandchildren, and on the third and on the fourth (generations)." The creed, as expressed in Exodus 34:7 and Numbers 14:18, presents an unresolved tension, in which divine mercy and divine justice are juxtaposed. The theological tension of Exodus 34:7 and Numbers 14:18 is engaged and explored through narratives within the Hebrew Bible that relate instances of forgiveness and vicarious punishment (2 Sam. 12:13–14), transgenerational reward (mercy), and punishment (1 Kings 15:1–4, 26–30), and individual punishment and pardon (Exod. 32:34; Num. 14:20–35), whether deferred or immediate. In this way, the *traditum* of the character creed is not simply repeated, but commented upon with multiple interpretations through the process of its transmission throughout the rest of the Hebrew Bible. Regardless of whether one sees the variety of exegetical applications of the creed in the Scriptures as contrastive or complementary, biblical writers regularly go beyond the simple repetition of the creed in their use of it. To account for the dexterity with which biblical writers selectively employ these character creedal statements and develop "deliberate exegetical modifications," Fishbane sees Exodus 34:6–7 as the authoritative model for the exegetical reuses of the phrase throughout the Hebrew Bible due to its complete form and "relative antiquity."[29] Whether Exodus 34:6–7 represents an inclusive, more mature and developed form of the character creed than the leaner text of Numbers 14:17–18, or vice versa, certainly Fishbane is right to observe that the narrative placement of Exodus 34:6–7 within the Pentateuch accords its form of the creed an authoritative status because, on the canonical ordering of the narrative, Numbers 14:17 assumes the divine revelation of Exodus 34:6–7. So what are readers to make of selective applications in Scripture of one or more of the discrete creedal elements, while ignoring

[29] Fishbane refers to Exod. 34:6–7 as the "divine attribute formulary." See *Biblical Interpretation in Ancient Israel*, 335.

or revising other elements? How does the *traditum* of Exodus 34:6–7 have ongoing authority when theological clarifications and explanations accrue throughout the Scripture in the development and revision of the creed? How can the *traditio*, the process of prophetic revision in the application of the creed to a specific community, participate in the authority of the *traditum*, which is seemingly set aside?

Refining Communal Creedal Interpretation: Ezekiel and Deuteronomy

Creedal statements in the Hebrew Bible such as Exodus 20:1, 4–6, and Numbers 14:18 are not only foundational faith statements and interpretive lenses that serve as literary building blocks for the structure and content of canonical Hebrew Scriptures. These creedal statements are themselves subject to editorial revision and theological clarification within the canon, prompting Bernard Levenson to characterize the revision of these foundational statements as a type of exegetical subversion.[30]

Levenson uses the language of exegetical subversion to describe the reception of Exodus 20:1–4 and its doctrine of "transgenerational punishment" elsewhere in the Hebrew Scriptures. The best-known example that Levenson examines is that found in Ezekiel 18:1–4 (see also Jeremiah 31:29–30):

> What do you mean by repeating this proverb concerning the land of Israel: "The parents [lit.: 'fathers'] have eaten sour grapes, and the children's teeth are set on edge"? As I live, says the Lord GOD, this proverb shall no more be used by you in Israel. Know that all lives are mine; the life of the parent as well as the life of the child is mine: it is only the person who sins that shall die. (NRSV)

[30] Levenson, "Human Voice in Revelation," 53.

The verses immediately following (Ezek. 18:5–29) form the most sustained argument in the Hebrew Bible against Judah's presumption of an unassailable doctrine of "transgenerational punishment," Levenson's term for what seems to be a straightforward and accurate exegesis of Exodus 20:5–6, and one consistent with the theological argument of 1 Kings 15.[31] The proverb, against which Ezekiel and Jeremiah proclaimed a doctrine of "individual punishment," was rooted in just such a straightforward exegetical tradition of Exodus 20:5–6's divinely revealed creed, "visiting the iniquity of the parents upon the children to the third and the fourth generation." According to Levenson, both Ezekiel and Jeremiah avoid direct alteration of Exodus 20:4–6 through their "radical innovation" of the proverb's "human voice" (tradition), rather than the "divine voice" (revelation) speaking in Exodus's decalogue. Ezekiel, on the other hand, evoking a statement from Deuteronomy, revises even further the transgenerational punishment emphasized in Exodus 20:4–6. Deuteronomy 7:9–10 retains the language of transgenerational favor for those who love God but promises individual punishment for each person who hates God (i.e., who refuses to keep the Torah):

> You know that the LORD your God, he is God, the trusted God who keeps covenant and faithful love for those who love him, those keeping his commandments, to a thousand generations—yet repaying to his face the one who hates him, by destroying him. He will not delay with one who hates him. He will repay him to his face.

---

[31]The historian blames the punishment of Israel and Judah not only on previous kings (e.g., Manasseh in 2 Kings 23:26) but also on the perpetuation of those sins by their contemporary descendants (2 Kings 24:9). Such a move seems to reflect Deuteronomy's own revision of the decalogue of Exod. 20:1–4. See Levenson, "The Human Voice in Revelation," 54–55.

The quotation style of Deuteronomy 7:9–10 indicates its dependence on Exodus 20:5–6, while the similar but different expressions and content in the Deuteronomy passage innovate the latter, revising or clarifying the transgenerational punishment therein. Levenson sees this Deuteronomic innovation to the creed as an entirely new, elegant, sophisticated, but tendentious reworking of Exodus 20:5–6:

> At a single bold stroke the authors of this text (i.e., Deut. 7:9–10) reject the authority of the Decalogue and justifying their legal innovation. . . . They invoke the authority of the older revelation only to subvert it, only to transfer its authority to their own new doctrine of individual responsibility.[32]

Based on the analysis of the creedal formulas within their broader narrative contexts presented herein, such clarification and revision of the theological content of the creedal statements may be noticed even within the narrative context in which they are embedded.

Conclusion

Fishbane's and Levenson's theses are provocative. While observed and declared complexities of textual development should be carefully examined, with a healthy awareness that other solutions may better explain a text's current structure and content, it would be hasty and unhelpful to dismiss Fishbane or Levenson out of hand or solely based on ideology. Restoration heirs have long held that Scripture is best interpreted through Scripture, and may concur with Fishbane that at times, the earliest commentary on Scripture is within Scripture itself. Thus one observes that in the authoritative interpretative traditions that appear in the literature of Second Temple Judaism—such as the *pesharim* (canonical commentaries)

[32] Levenson, "The Human Voice in Revelation," 54–55.

from Qumran—later communities grant their exegetical interpretations an authoritative status.[33] Indeed, the *pesharim* provide evidence for a strategy of biblical interpretation that is paralleled in the New Testament. As Christians, we confess, recite, and have canonized our community's authoritative interpretations (*traditio*) of the Hebrew Scriptures (*traditum*). One can see this same principle in Rabbinic Judaism's Midrashic expansions of *haggadic* literature, and developed *halakhic* applications and interpretations. Clearly, in the case of the New Testament, interpretative commentary on the received Scriptures of the Hebrew Bible, guided by the Holy Spirit, becomes authoritative and eventually becomes canonized Scripture. The emphasis for the thesis here is similar to that of Levenson: even within the canon of the Hebrew Bible, interpretative commentary, supplied by later interpretive communities, is contained within Scripture itself.[34] Thus the community and the canon stand in a complementary relationship with each other. The divine authority of the canon is imparted to the community via their submission to it. The influence of the community is discernible because the Scriptures are shaped by it and the canon(s) that it preserves.

---

[33] For example, 1QpHab II, 1–2.

[34] See more generally J. Neusner, *Rabbinic Literature and the New Testament: What We Cannot Show, We Do Not Know* (Valley Forge, PA: Trinity Press International, 1994; repr., Eugene, OR: Wipf & Stock, 2004), 21–40. Neusner has observed that if Christianity had progressed on a path similar to Rabbinic Judaism, the transmission of the New Testament would flow in a single stream, along with the exegesis and commentary of its earliest interpreters.

2

Understanding Scripture through Apostolic Proclamation

J. David Stark

Biblical scholarship has begun to recognize more explicitly that early Christian beliefs legitimately shaped how the earliest members of the Jesus movement interpreted their Scriptures.[1] According to what has been called a "dispositional account of belief," such beliefs have natural and inevitable extensions for

[1] For example, Matthew W. Bates, *The Hermeneutics of the Apostolic Proclamation: The Center of Paul's Method of Scriptural Interpretation* (Waco, TX: Baylor University Press, 2012); J. David Stark, *Sacred Texts and Paradigmatic Revolutions: The Hermeneutical Worlds of the Qumran Sectarian Manuscripts and the Letter to the Romans*, Jewish and Christian Texts in Contexts and Related Studies 16 (New York: Bloomsbury T&T Clark, 2013). For their comments on earlier drafts, I am particularly grateful to Noemí Palomares of Boston College and Floyd Parker of Faulkner University.

their communities.[2] First Corinthians 15 provides an ideal case study in the influence of these dispositional beliefs on readings of Scripture within the early Jesus movement. The chapter begins with a summary of proclaimed belief (vv. 3b–5), which is followed by a discussion of bodily resurrection that includes a multifaceted interaction with Scripture.

Particularly to be examined here are Paul's scriptural quotations in vv. 25 (Ps. 109:1 OG; Ps. 110:1 ET, HB), 27 (Ps. 8:7 HB, OG; 8:6 ET), 32 (Isa. 22:13), 45 (Gen. 2:7), and 54–55 (Isa. 25:8; Hosea 13:14). Careful analysis of these quotations shows the prism-like effect that dispositional beliefs had in fostering the early Jesus movement's interaction with Scripture. By placing Scripture within this dispositional prism, Paul shows how Scripture refracts into a spectrum of testimony about bodily resurrection. Of course, as with light moving through a prism, so too for Paul, this refraction makes Scripture's testimony not something other than itself. Rather, it separates out this testimony more clearly into individual spectrums that the testimony already contains.

Belief: Assertion or Disposition?

When discussing belief, many are quite comfortable answering questions like "Who do you believe in?" or "What do you believe?" Probably less immediately intelligible are questions like "How (i.e., in what manner) do you believe?" or, still more, "Where or when do you believe?" Such questions show how understanding belief as an act of assertion fails to provide a fully adequate account of the kind of action belief is. Does one believe simply by believing or, at most, by being sure about what one hopes for and certain about what one does not see (Heb. 11:1)—although these definitions are hardly more specific? Does one believe always and in all

[2]For example, H. H. Price, *Belief*, Muirhead Library of Philosophy (London: Allen & Unwin, 1969); Anthony C. Thiselton, *The Hermeneutics of Doctrine* (Grand Rapids: Eerdmans, 2007).

places? If we think so but understand belief as an act of assertion, how do we know that we still believe in the Father, Son, and Holy Spirit, even when we are asleep or unconscious?[3] If we understand belief as an assertion of some proposition, then difficulties like these arise. This is even true if it is granted that the belief asserted should affect one's behavior. Is not the line between asserting and behaving itself rather blurry and indefinite?[4]

We can try to avoid these difficulties by identifying a different way of understanding the types of actions that are involved with belief. Stemming from H. H. Price's work, Anthony Thiselton describes a "dispositional account of belief," or an account of belief as a disposition rather than an assertion.[5] In such an account, belief is "inextricably embodied in patterns of habit, commitment, and action, which constitute endorsement, 'backing,' or 'surroundings'" for belief.[6] Statements in the form "I believe . . ." or "we believe . . ." are not primarily descriptive or informational.[7] Instead, they nail colors to the mast for oneself or one's community. They commit the speakers to "respond to situations both by expressing and 'standing behind' belief utterances in situations that challenge belief, or that demand action appropriate to belief."[8]

Thus, "belief . . . is action-oriented . . . and embedded in the particularities and contingencies of everyday living"; it involves a "moral and volitional dimension" and the "formation of character."[9] For instance, "a relation with God the Father contributes . . . 'surroundings' that give currency to claims to believe in the Son[, and] to declare settled belief in Christ . . . can retain no working currency if the speaker . . . chooses the path of sin and alienation from

[3] See Thiselton, *Hermeneutics of Doctrine*, 19–20.
[4] Thiselton, *Hermeneutics of Doctrine*, 19–20.
[5] Thiselton, *Hermeneutics of Doctrine*, 19–42.
[6] Thiselton, *Hermeneutics of Doctrine*, 20, 28–29.
[7] Thiselton, *Hermeneutics of Doctrine*, 20, 33.
[8] Thiselton, *Hermeneutics of Doctrine*, 21, 29–30.
[9] Thiselton, *Hermeneutics of Doctrine*, 21.

God."[10] In this case, the problem is not merely that the behavior is inconsistent with the declared belief. The behavior actually affirms something contrary to the declared belief because the behavior has supplied different attendant circumstances than the declared belief requires.[11] A first-person declaration of belief has entailments that stretch beyond that declaration's content. Yet *these entailments are not something other than the declaration*, any more than a person who "nails her colors to the mast" is different from the arm that swings the hammer or any more than someone who "takes a stand" is something other than the legs on which he does so.[12]

If we contextualize belief in this concrete way, there is further reason to consider carefully this belief's attendant "backing" or "surroundings." That is, try as we might to excavate (proto-)creedal statements in biblical or other early Christian literature, we risk translating these commitments into freestanding assertions rather than the answers they are to specific questions that have arisen in particular contexts.[13] And the danger of this translation is precisely that of nullifying the excavated commitments.

For instance, the doctrine of the Trinity is not merely a set of mostly superfluous reflections on divine ontology.[14] But it is often

---

[10] Thiselton, *Hermeneutics of Doctrine*, 25.

[11] Thiselton, *Hermeneutics of Doctrine*, 19, 25–26.

[12] Cf. Thiselton, *Hermeneutics of Doctrine*, 26, 28.

[13] Cf. Thiselton, *Hermeneutics of Doctrine*, 38–39; see also Hans-Georg Gadamer, *Truth and Method*, ed. and trans. Joel Weinsheimer and Donald G. Marshall, 2nd ed., Bloomsbury Revelations (London: Bloomsbury Academic, 2013), 370–87. In referencing "(proto-)creedal statements," I am highlighting the "in between" level of standardization of certain New Testament texts. The formulations in such texts are unlikely to be strictly occasional, but these formulations do not reflect the same kind of standardization as later creeds. Whatever terminology is employed, however, 1 Corinthians 15:3b–5 draws upon a common tradition of apostolic proclamation and makes this proclamation a basis for the following argument.

[14] For another example too lengthy to include here, see J. David Stark, "The Problem with Doctrines as Freestanding Assertions," *J. David Stark* (blog), July 15, 2019, https://www.jdavidstark.com/the-problem-with-doctrines-as-freestanding-assertions/.

treated this way when it becomes a freestanding problem rather than an answer to a question that arises and provokes a response. By contrast, for Irenaeus, the doctrine of the Trinity answers—among others—the quite specific question of the goodness of the material creation. Faced with opposition from various gnosticisms, Irenaeus articulates a contrary doctrine of the true God's oneness: the creator God is the father of the Lord Messiah Jesus, and these two with the Holy Spirit are intimately involved with and affirming of the created order.[15] The heresy does not precede the orthodoxy.[16] Rather, the heresy provokes into action a faith that already exhibits a "disposition to respond."[17]

To summarize then, a dispositional account of belief highlights how integral belief is to the horizon that gives rise to it. Belief can, however, still be shared. Thus it is possible to translate a belief's required backing from one horizon into another or, as in conversion, to move into a shared horizon where a given belief has currency. These dynamics mean that studying the beliefs of the early Jesus movement requires more than excavating doctrinal assertions. The surroundings, or horizon, within which such beliefs were nurtured also bear careful attention.

The same goes for the study of the early Jesus movement's scriptural interpretation. This attention properly involves a whole host of issues, and much broader work needs to be done. But even in itself, 1 Corinthians 15 provides a good deal of information about the dispositional character of belief within the early Jesus movement and how this belief shaped the movement's scriptural interpretation.

---

[15] For example, Irenaeus, *Against Heresies*, §§1.22.1, 2.28.1–2, 3.9 2–3, 3.11.1, 4.35.4.

[16] Contra, for example, Walter Bauer, *Orthodoxy and Heresy in Earliest Christianity*, ed. Robert A. Kraft and Gerhard Krodel (Philadelphia: Fortress, 1971), 28–29.

[17] Thiselton, *Hermeneutics of Doctrine*, 21, 37.

Belief Asserted (1 Corinthians 15:1–11)

At the beginning of 1 Corinthians 15 stands a summary of some of the most important elements (ἐν πρώτοις) in the early Jesus movement's preaching.[18] The message is Paul's, but it is also proclaimed more generally. Paul "received" the message from others who also preached it (1 Cor. 15:3a, 11b). And part of what Paul likely received is a summary of the key components of the message that he rehearses in 1 Corinthians 15:3b–5.[19] These are "that the Messiah died in behalf of our sins according to the Scriptures and that he was buried and that he was raised on the third day according to the Scriptures and that he appeared to Cephas, then to the twelve" (1 Cor. 15:3b–5).[20] This core testimony is then buttressed by Jesus's appearance to the five hundred, to James and the apostles, and to Paul himself (1 Cor. 15:6–8). Both Paul's shift to "then" at the start of 1 Corinthians 15:6 and his additional reference to the "apostles" in v. 7 suggest that, with v. 6, Paul is moving away from the primary content of the proclamation of the early Jesus movement and toward supplementary information.[21]

---

[18] Walter Bauer et al., eds., *A Greek-English Lexicon of the New Testament and Other Early Christian Literature*, trans. Frederick W. Danker, 3rd ed. (Chicago: University of Chicago Press, 2000), s.v. πρῶτος §2.a.α; Anthony C. Thiselton, *The First Epistle to the Corinthians: A Commentary on the Greek Text*, New International Greek Testament Commentary (Grand Rapids: Eerdmans, 2000), 1186. Quotations of the Greek New Testament accord with Eberhard Nestle et al., eds., *Novum Testamentum Graece*, 28th ed. (Stuttgart: Deutsche Bibelgesellschaft, 2013).

[19] See, for example, Hans Conzelmann, *1 Corinthians: A Commentary on the First Epistle to the Corinthians*, trans. James W. Leitch, Hermeneia (Philadelphia: Fortress, 1975), 251–55; Michael R. Licona, *The Resurrection of Jesus: A New Historiographical Approach* (Downers Grove, IL: InterVarsity Press, 2010), 223–35.

[20] Translations are the author's.

[21] See Bates, *Hermeneutics of the Apostolic Proclamation*, 62–63; Conzelmann, *1 Corinthians*, 258; Jerome Murphy-O'Connor, "Tradition and Redaction in 1 Cor. 15:3–7," *Catholic Biblical Quarterly* 43, no. 4 (1981): 582–89; Thiselton, *First Epistle to the Corinthians*, 1188–89, 1200–1203, 1205–6.

In this summary, the double affirmation that the message is "according to the Scriptures" reinforces its connection with what the early Jesus movement received as the divine word in written form. Nevertheless, it is difficult to identify where Israel's Scriptures clearly set out the Messiah's death on the behalf of sins and resurrection on the third day (1 Cor. 15:3–4). Thus the reference may not be to particularly identifiable texts but to a composite of Israel's Scriptures when read in a certain way.[22]

In any case, in 1 Corinthians 15, Paul nowhere justifies that Jesus's death and resurrection are "according to the Scriptures," as asserted in vv. 3–4. Instead, Paul presumes the Corinthians accept the scriptural interpretation on these two points that was embedded in prior preaching (cf. vv. 1–2, 11). Therefore, in 1 Corinthians 15, where Paul mentions Jesus's death and resurrection, he reasons *from* these scripturally situated events to develop his argument. Along the way, this development interweaves the interpretation of still further scriptural texts.

By comparison with a "dispositional account of belief," another set of features in 1 Corinthians 15:1–11 also bears attention. In vv. 1–3 and 11, Paul stresses his and others' personal involvement with the proclamation of the message delivered to the Corinthians.[23] This act was part of how they enacted the "disposition to respond" inherent in their belief. It was their "nailing their colors to the mast," "taking a stand," and going on record in support of Jesus's messianic claims. As such, only just beneath the surface of Paul's account of this proclamation is his own testimony of first-person belief and commitment to backing the message he helped proclaim.[24]

---

[22] Bates, *Hermeneutics of the Apostolic Proclamation*, 65–67, 71–72; cf. Thiselton, *First Epistle to the Corinthians*, 1190, 1195. See also Luke 24:13–49 and its brief discussion in Thiselton, *First Epistle to the Corinthians*, 1189.

[23] Cf. Bates, *Hermeneutics of the Apostolic Proclamation*, 73–74.

[24] Thiselton, *First Epistle to the Corinthians*, 1187–89.

Similarly, in vv. 1–2 and 11, Paul reminds the Corinthians about how they have variously "received," "taken [their] stand in," or "believed" this message and how, therefore, they need to "hold fast" to it (see also 1 Cor. 15:58).[25] Paul's descriptions are unavoidably second-person, but they bring the Corinthians to a fresh awareness of their own *first*-person faith commitments.[26] As first-person commitments, they cannot easily be rejected. For the Corinthians, their belief also creates a "disposition to respond." And Paul judges that a reminder about this belief will trigger fresh loyalty to the basis he lays out for his following discussion.[27]

In sum, 1 Corinthians 15:3b–5 encapsulates the message Paul and others proclaimed. This summary reminds the Corinthians of the teaching they received. As such, they had not merely heard this message but had also accepted it as true. By highlighting their common commitment to this message—through preaching on the one hand and through acceptance on the other—1 Corinthians 15:1–11 brings to the surface the "disposition to respond" that lies within the belief that Paul and the Corinthians share. This is particularly true with Paul and the Corinthians' common acceptance that "the Messiah . . . was raised" (1 Cor. 15:3b–4). First Corinthians 15:1–11 then provides a working foundation for the argument that

---

[25] Cf. Bates, *Hermeneutics of the Apostolic Proclamation*, 74.

[26] Thiselton, *Hermeneutics of Doctrine*, 1184.

[27] Thiselton declines to understand Paul's initial γνωρίζω . . . ὑμῖν fully in the sense of "I remind you" (1 Cor. 15:1). *First Epistle to the Corinthians*, 1183. To Thiselton's point, 1 Corinthians 15 does disclose things that the Corinthians had not yet understood sufficiently. At the same time, Paul couches the new disclosures in terms of a reminder about "the gospel that I preached to you, which also you received." See also Friedrich Blass, Albert Debrunner, and Robert Walter Funk, *A Greek Grammar of the New Testament and Other Early Christian Literature* (Chicago: University of Chicago Press, 1961), §§318, 332; Gordon Fee, *The First Epistle to the Corinthians*, rev. ed., New International Commentary on the New Testament (Grand Rapids: Eerdmans, 2014), 842; Daniel B. Wallace, *Greek Grammar beyond the Basics: An Exegetical Syntax of the New Testament* (Grand Rapids: Zondervan, 1996), 555–58; Thiselton, *First Epistle to the Corinthians*, 1185, 1188–89, 1217.

follows. As such, it prepares the way both for Paul to continue responding to what might jeopardize the Corinthians' faith in the resurrection and for the Corinthians themselves to accept afresh both the general belief that "the Messiah . . . was raised" (1 Cor. 15:3b–4) and this belief's additional entailments.[28]

Scripture Refracted through Interpretive Dispositions

The balance of 1 Corinthians 15 contains Paul's closely argued defense of the resurrection.[29] After vv. 1–11, the chapter divides into three parts.[30] Verses 12–34 argue for a general resurrection to be experienced by Jesus's followers. Verses 35–53 explain the nature of the resurrection, especially regarding the kinds of bodies with which the Corinthians can anticipate being raised.[31] Verses 54–58 then conclude the argument and encourage the Corinthians to remain true to the testimony that Paul has delivered to them. Of particular interest is how Paul understands Scripture as refracting into these sections. In each of Paul's appeals to Scripture, the hermeneutic force of the Messiah's resurrection (1 Cor. 15:3b–4) can be discerned as part of the prism through which Paul reads these texts and refracts them into support for his view of the resurrection.[32]

---

[28] Cf. Thiselton, *First Epistle to the Corinthians*, 1184–86.

[29] The reason for this defense cannot be described much more confidently than to say that some at Corinth questioned or denied one or more components of Paul's view of the resurrection. See Thiselton, *First Epistle to the Corinthians*, 1172–78.

[30] On treating 1 Corinthians 15 as having this somewhat longer conclusion, see Dietrich-Alex Koch, *Die Schrift als Zeuge des Evangeliums: Untersuchungen zur Verwendung und zum Verständnis der Schrift bei Paulus*, Beiträge zur historischen Theologie 69 (Tübingen: Mohr Siebeck, 1986), 107; Christopher D. Stanley, *Paul and the Language of Scripture: Citation Technique in the Pauline Epistles and Contemporary Literature*, Society for New Testament Studies Monograph Series 74 (Cambridge: Cambridge University Press, 1992), 212.

[31] Contra Thiselton, *First Epistle to the Corinthians*, 1178.

[32] Cf. Bates, *Hermeneutics of the Apostolic Proclamation*, 64–65.

Spectrum 1: Why a Resurrection?

In justifying a bodily resurrection, Paul appeals to Psalms and Isaiah. The appeal from Psalms 109:1 (OG; 110:1 ET, HB) and 8:7 (HB, OG; 8:6 ET) comes in 1 Corinthians 15:25 and 27. The appeal from Isaiah 22:13 comes in 1 Corinthians 15:32.

Psalms 109:1 (OG; 110:1 ET, HB) and 8:7 (HB, OG; 8:6 ET) in 1 Corinthians 15:25 and 27. Verse 24 describes how, at "the end," the Messiah "will deliver over the kingdom to his God and Father when he destroys every rule and every authority and power." This assertion's backing follows in v. 25: "for it is necessary for him to reign until he puts all his enemies under his feet." In v. 24, the messianic Son exercises authority until he delivers it to his Father. According to v. 25, this authority must continue until it is perfected in the Son's having "all his enemies under his feet."

The description of how the enemies get "under his feet" falls on the border between indirect quotation and paraphrase.[33] The base text is Psalm 109:1 (OG; 110:1 ET, HB). By comparison with this text in the Göttingen Septuagint,[34] Paul has made a minor grammatical accommodation from "I will put" to "he will put," has shifted "your enemies" to "all his enemies," and has removed an explicit characterization of the enemies as constituting a "footstool."[35] The enemies are still underfoot, and Paul may well conceive of them there as a "footstool" (cf. Matt. 24:44). But there seems to be no great difference in the emphasis of the text in either case.[36] And with or without explicit reference to a "footstool,"

---

[33]See Stark, *Sacred Texts and Paradigmatic Revolutions*, 47–49.

[34]The "Göttingen Septuagint" is the major critical edition of the Greek translation of the Old Testament. Robert Hanhart et al., eds., *Septuaginta: Vetus Testamentum Graecum* (Göttingen: Vandenhoeck & Ruprecht, 1931–).

[35]In Fee's opinion, 1 Cor. 15:25 "is *not* a citation but an adaptation of the psalm," but he grants that "the allusion[is] certain." *First Epistle to the Corinthians*, 836n187, 837n194; italics original.

[36]On the metaphor, see Roy E. Ciampa and Brian S. Rosner, *The First Letter to the Corinthians*, Pillar New Testament Commentary (Grand Rapids:

Paul's use of Psalm 109:1 (OG; 110:1 ET, HB) strongly resonates with the theme of the messianic victory over death that swells in 1 Corinthians 15:54–57.

Who puts the enemies under whose feet is technically ambiguous. Both the Father and the Son have been suggested in both positions.[37] For evidence that might help determine the subject of the verb "puts," Gordon Fee summarizes:

> In favor of "Christ" is (a) the grammar itself, since the natural antecedent is the subject of the preceding "he must reign," referring to Christ; and (b) the fact that this serves as an explanation of the preceding sentence (v. 24), where Christ is the subject of the clause "when he destroys all dominion, etc." In favor of "God" is (a) the fact that in the psalm itself God places all things under the Messiah's feet, and (b) that in the concluding sentence (v. 28) God is finally designated as the subject of the citation from the Psalter (8:6), that is, as the one who has subjected all things to Christ. Almost certainly we must go with the grammar here and see Christ as the subject.[38]

In a note, Fee presses the weight of the grammatical evidence in favor of "Christ" as the subject on the grounds that this is *not* a citation but an adaptation of the psalm to Paul's own grammar, and a reader (or hearer) could not possibly have understood "God" to be the subject until he or she came to v. 27c. Had Paul intended

---

Eerdmans, 2010), 772; Hans-Joachim Kraus, *Psalms 60–150*, trans. Hilton C. Oswald, Continental Commentaries (Minneapolis: Fortress, 1993), 349.

[37] Hanhart et al., eds., *Septuaginta*. The shift from "your enemies" to "all his enemies" likely happens partly because Psalm 8:7 (HB, OG; 8:6 ET) references "all things" being underfoot. Ciampa and Rosner, *First Letter to the Corinthians*, 771; Fee, *First Epistle to the Corinthians*, 837n189.

[38] Fee, *First Epistle to the Corinthians*, 837; see also Thiselton, *First Epistle to the Corinthians*, 1233–34.

"God" at this point, it is almost demanded grammatically that he would have inserted a direct reference to "God."[39]

Precisely following the referents for all of Paul's pronouns in this paragraph is difficult. But there seem to be several good reasons that Fee does not mention for understanding the Father to be the one who puts the enemies "under [the Son's] feet" (1 Cor. 15:25).[40] First, Fee recognizes that 1 Corinthians 15:25–28 forms a coherent argumentative unit.[41] Yet he also admits that his reading of this unit requires a shift in roles at v. 27a.[42] By contrast, if one understands the Father to be the one who subjects enemies to the Son in v. 25, then no shift is required within vv. 25–28. This reading does require a shift in the subject of the verb between vv. 24 and 25, as Fee notes. But there seems to be no good reason that a change in pronominal referent between vv. 24 and 25 would be any less likely than one between vv. 26 and 27.

Second, in favor of understanding v. 25 as referring to the Son who subjects enemies to himself, Fee cites a grammatical linkage with v. 24.[43] But seeing this grammatical linkage presupposes that "a reader (or hearer) could not possibly have understood 'God' to be the subject" in v. 25.[44] The difficulty with this assumption arises because Psalm 109:1 (OG; 110:1 ET, HB) was such a prominent text for the early Jesus movement's messianic reflection.[45] This prominence is especially relevant in two ways:

1. Several New Testament texts quote or allude to Psalm 109:1 (OG; 110:1 ET, HB). Excluding 1 Corinthians 15:25,

---

[39] Fee, *First Epistle to the Corinthians*, 837n194; cf. Gordon Fee, *Pauline Christology: An Exegetical-Theological Study* (Peabody, MA: Hendrickson, 2007), 107–14.

[40] See Ciampa and Rosner, *First Letter to the Corinthians*, 772.

[41] Fee, *First Epistle to the Corinthians*, 836.

[42] Fee, *Pauline Christology*, 112–13.

[43] Fee, *First Epistle to the Corinthians*, 837; Fee, *Pauline Christology*, 109, 111.

[44] Fee, *First Epistle to the Corinthians*, 837n194.

[45] Fee, *First Epistle to the Corinthians*, 836n187.

wherever it can be determined who the text portrays as doing the "putting under the Messiah's feet," the reference is *never* to the Messiah's own subjection of his enemies (see Mark 12:35–37 and parallels; Acts 2:34; Eph. 1:20–21; Heb. 1:3).[46] By contrast, on Fee's reading, 1 Corinthians 15:25 would give a different interpretation of Psalm 109:1 (OG; 110:1 ET, HB) than occurs anywhere else in the New Testament.

2. Specifically within the Pauline corpus and on Fee's own accounting, Psalm 109:1 (OG; 110:1 ET, HB) is also referenced in Romans 8:34, Colossians 3:1, and Ephesians 1:20.[47] Romans 8:34 and Colossians 3:1 only describe how the psalm situates the Messiah at Yahweh's right hand. But Ephesians 1:20–23 implies that the Messiah is put there by another figure and, in that position, finds himself over all things (see Eph. 1:15–23). Ephesians 1:20–23 also has a further similarity to the structure of 1 Corinthians 15:25–27. Following the allusion to Psalm 109:1 (OG; 110:1 ET, HB) in Ephesians 1:20–21, Ephesians 1:22 also quotes Psalm 8:7 (HB, OG; 8:6 ET), just as 1 Corinthians 15:27. Therefore, this pairing of these two Psalmic texts needs to be added to the one Fee notes in Hebrews 1:13 and 2:6–9.[48] If Ephesians and Hebrews both combine Psalms 8 and 109 (OG) to speak about the Father's subjecting all things to the Son, then a similar function in 1 Corinthians 15 becomes still more likely.

---

[46] Cf. Nestle et al., *Novum Testamentum*, 854. Hebrews 10:12–13 does not explicitly say who makes the enemies into a footstool. But the passive verb and the prior reference in Hebrews 1:3 suggest that the Father does this for the Messiah. Thus this text also would fit the general pattern outlined previously.

[47] Fee, *Pauline Christology*, 114.

[48] Fee, *First Epistle to the Corinthians*, 836n187.

Consequently, due to the prominence of Psalm 109:1 (OG; 110:1 ET, HB) and the consistency of its interpretation elsewhere on the issue of who does the subjecting, it is likely that 1 Corinthians 15:25 follows this pattern. Particularly if Psalm 109:1 (OG; 110:1 ET, HB) is—as it seems to be elsewhere in the New Testament—a "stock text," then Fee's premise that "a reader (or hearer) could not possibly have understood 'God' to be the subject" becomes doubtful. For example, in both Hebrew and Greek, 2 Chronicles 30:27 refers to "his holy dwelling place in heaven." Verbally expressed in the context, the only referents for the pronoun "his" are Solomon, David, and perhaps Israel (v. 26). Yet the "holy dwelling place in heaven" belongs not to any of these but to Yahweh. The phraseology "holy dwelling place in heaven" is sufficient to identify the referent of "his," even without verbally including this referent in the context (cf. Deut. 26:15; Ps. 68:5; Isa. 63:15). Similarly, it should not be surprising that Paul expected the Corinthians to understand his reference to Psalm 109:1 (OG; 110:1 ET, HB) as repeating the typical interpretation that situated the Father as the one doing the subjecting. Within this context, Paul's use of Psalm 109:1 (OG; 110:1 ET, HB) is entirely explicable.

More distinctive is his interpretation that "death, the last enemy, is being made powerless" (1 Cor. 15:26).[49] This interpretation involves two hermeneutic movements. First and most obviously, Paul classifies "death" as one of the Messiah's enemies. Twice in Paul's argument, he refers to the Messiah as the one who "makes alive" (1 Cor. 15:22, 45). Death opposes this "making alive" and finds itself among the Messiah's enemies.[50] As such, death is bound to be put "under his feet." Second, Paul figuratively renders death's being put under the Son's feet in terms of its "being made

[49] On the difficulty of satisfactorily translating this sentence, see Fee, *First Epistle to the Corinthians*, 838; Thiselton, *First Epistle to the Corinthians*, 1234–35.

[50] Thiselton, *First Epistle to the Corinthians*, 1280.

powerless." This interpretation is thoroughly in keeping with the tenor of the original psalmic metaphor.

But precisely how this interpretation relates to the following quotation from Psalm 8:7 (HB, OG; 8:6 ET) is not immediately clear. The putting of things "under [someone's] feet" is common between this quotation and that of Psalm 109:1 (OG; 110:1 ET, HB). The primary difference is that Psalm 109:1 (OG; 110:1 ET, HB) focuses specifically on "enemies," whereas Psalm 8:7 (HB, OG; 8:6 ET) addresses "all things." Following his quotation of Psalm 8:7 (HB, OG; 8:6 ET) in 1 Corinthians 15:27a, Paul continues to reflect on how "all things" become subject to the Son. Thus the quotation in v. 27a supports Paul's interpretation in v. 26 because it demonstrates something still more comprehensive than the narrower point of v. 26.[51]

In v. 27a, Paul's use of Psalm 8:7 (HB, OG; 8:6 ET) is more of an indirect quotation but still one with paraphrastic tendencies: "he has subjected all things under his feet."[52] By comparison with the Göttingen text, Paul has only adjusted the person of the verb ("you" to "he") and made a minor adjustment from one preposition (ὑποκάτω) to another synonymous one (ὑπό), with an attendant modification in the case of the preposition's object (genitive to accusative).[53] Here, again, it has been a point of debate whether the Father or the Son is the one who "has subjected all things."[54] According to v. 28, the Son is to become subject "to the one who subjected to him all things." This description of the Son as having had *someone else* subject "to him all things" suggests that, in v. 27a also, "all things" are put under the Son's feet by the Father.[55]

[51] Thiselton, *First Epistle to the Corinthians*, 1235–36.

[52] Stark, *Sacred Texts and Paradigmatic Revolutions*, 47–49.

[53] Stanley, *Paul and the Language of Scripture*, 206–7; Thiselton, *First Epistle to the Corinthians*, 1235.

[54] Thiselton, *First Epistle to the Corinthians*, 1235–36.

[55] Fee, *First Epistle to the Corinthians*, 839–42; Thiselton, *First Epistle to the Corinthians*, 1236.

Thus, similarly to v. 25, the Son is the main subject of the psalm (cf. Heb. 2:6–9). Paul has also absolutized the sense of "all things" such that it figuratively extends beyond the sense explicitly assigned to this phrase in the psalm (see Ps. 8:7–9 HB, OG; 8:6–8 ET).[56] Of course, Paul immediately adds that the scope of "all things" does not mean that the Father also becomes subject to the Son (1 Cor. 15:27b). Rather, the Son receives dominion over all creation and then subjects himself and his dominion to the Father (1 Cor. 15:24, 28).[57]

The result is that "God [the Father] should be all in all" (1 Cor. 15:28). The reference to being "all in all" has been variously interpreted. In this context, it refers to the Father's exercise of unopposed dominion over all creation (1 Cor. 15:24).[58] This sense is consistent with what similar language communicates elsewhere (e.g., Eph. 1:23; Col. 3:11).[59] In the end, the Son causes all things to submit to the Father's rule.

Given this understanding of this portion of Paul's argument, what connections can be discerned with his earlier summary of the early Jesus movement's proclamation and belief? What corollary responses emerge from the exegetical challenges of these verses? First, as already noted, death opposes the Messiah's task

---

[56] See Hans-Joachim Kraus, *Psalms 1–59*, trans. Hilton C. Oswald, Continental Commentaries (Minneapolis: Fortress, 1993), 183–85.

[57] Fee rightly suggests that the Son's subordination as envisioned in this passage is probably not eternal (and ontological?) but salvation-historical and functional. Fee, *Pauline Christology*, 113–14. See also A. T. Robertson and Alfred Plummer, *A Critical and Exegetical Commentary on the First Epistle of St Paul to the Corinthians*, 2nd ed., International Critical Commentary (1914; repr., Edinburgh: T&T Clark, 1929), 355; Thiselton, *First Epistle to the Corinthians*, 1231, 1237–38.

[58] C. K. Barrett, *The First Epistle to the Corinthians*, Black's New Testament Commentary (London: Continuum, 1968), 361; Conzelmann, *1 Corinthians*, 275; cf. Fee, *First Epistle to the Corinthians*, 841; see also Chrysostom, *Hom. 1 Cor.* 39.11.

[59] See also Stanley E. Porter, *Idioms of the Greek New Testament*, 2nd ed., Biblical Languages: Greek 2 (Sheffield: Sheffield Academic Press, 1999), 156–57.

of "making alive" and, as such, is his "last enemy [to be] made powerless." Yet Paul's rehearsal of the early Jesus movement's proclamation nowhere connects the Messiah's own resurrection to that of his followers. Jesus's death "on behalf of our sins" is the only element explicitly described as connected to Paul and the Corinthians in 1 Corinthians 15:3b–5.[60] It might have been necessary for the Messiah to rise from the dead to vindicate him and show that his ministry and death were approved by Israel's God. But why should the Messiah's rising from the dead also imply his task of "making alive" his dead followers? Other dead persons brought back to life occasioned no similar hope.

Paul does not qualify Jesus's resurrection as "on behalf of our resurrection" or something similar. But belief in and commitment to Jesus's resurrection entail this further response (cf. Rom. 4:23–25). Hoping in the Messiah "in this life only" will leave the Corinthians as the "most pitiable of all people" (1 Cor. 15:19). There is no middle ground allowed for the Messiah only to have been raised without his followers' resurrection following immediately behind it: "if the dead are not to be raised, the Messiah has not even been raised" (1 Cor. 15:16).[61] Thus the Messiah's own headship and becoming alive again make him the one who sets death at naught and enlivens those who cast their hopes on him both for the present life and for the one to come.

In addition, 1 Corinthians 15:3b–5 explicitly includes neither Jesus's ascension and session at the Father's right hand nor the participation in this dominion by Jesus's followers. Yet the risen Son now rules (1 Cor. 15:23–28). And, as becomes clearer later in the chapter, part of what it means for Jesus's followers to be raised as he

---

[60] This phrasing may well already have been traditional by the time Paul wrote 1 Corinthians. Thiselton, *First Epistle to the Corinthians*, 1191.

[61] Cf. Fee, *First Epistle to the Corinthians*, 837–38; N. T. Wright, *The Climax of the Covenant: Christ and the Law in Pauline Theology* (Edinburgh: T&T Clark, 1991), 41–55.

was is that they share his dominion—specifically that over his last enemy, death (1 Cor. 15:26, 54–57). Thus, although 1 Corinthians 15:3b–5 nowhere explicitly includes this information, Paul's following discussion clarifies that he understands these implications to be necessary extensions of the claim that "the Messiah . . . was raised" (1 Cor. 15:3b–4).

Isaiah 22:13 in 1 Corinthians 15:32. The following section in 1 Corinthians 15 provides an indirect but exact quotation of Isaiah 22:13, according to the Göttingen text: "Let us eat and drink, for tomorrow, we die" (1 Cor. 15:32).[62] In making this quotation, Paul figures himself and his addressees into the position of the group that Isaiah exhorts. Whatever the significance of the reference to "those who are being baptized on behalf of the dead" in 1 Corinthians 15:29,[63] the following vv. 30–32a clearly rehearse the varieties of difficulties encountered by Paul, his associates, and perhaps the Corinthians themselves.

Presumably, they all have some reason for enduring these difficulties. But "if the dead are not raised," this reason does not prove valid. Instead, a different course of action legitimates itself—namely, eating and drinking in view of a soon-coming death (1 Cor. 15:32). This logic suggests that the reason for enduring the difficulties mentioned is the hope of a future resurrection. The difficulties themselves entail no benefit (1 Cor. 15:32a). But when undertaken in faithfulness to the Messiah and in hope of the coming resurrection, these difficulties become steps toward that destination.

These ethical implications are part of the "backing" to be supplied in keeping with the proclamation of the early Jesus movement that "the Messiah . . . was raised" (1 Cor. 15:3b–4). It makes no

---

[62] Stark, *Sacred Texts and Paradigmatic Revolutions*, 48.

[63] For an underappreciated option in interpreting this text, see J. David Stark, "Baptism on Behalf of the Dead at Corinth—and in the Pentateuch?," in *Scripture, Texts, and Tracings in 1 Corinthians*, ed. Linda L. Belleville and B. J. Oropeza, Scripture and Paul (Lanham, MD: Lexington, 2019), 161–86.

sense for the Messiah's followers to take up their lives with eating and drinking if they are to experience resurrection. Instead, such people should willingly encounter "danger every hour," "die daily," and "f[ight] with wild animals" (1 Cor. 15:30–32).

Paul does not state it directly, but this argument presupposes that the life given in resurrection is better than the life experienced at present (cf. 1 Cor. 15:42–57). If the resurrection life were of poorer quality, presumably it would still be legitimate to "eat and drink" with little care given to the life to come. If the two kinds of life were of roughly equal quality, then the claims of "eat[ing] and drink[ing]" might be of roughly equal strength as those of encountering "danger every hour," "d[ying] daily," and "f[ighting] with wild animals." Yet Paul clearly represents "eat[ing] and drink[ing]" as a worse option and urges a willingness to endure difficulties while hoping for the future resurrection (1 Cor. 15:33–34).

Spectrum 2: What Kind of Resurrection? (Gen. 2:7 in 1 Cor. 15:45)

In vv. 35–53, Paul describes how resurrection life is better than the present kind of life.[64] It is so, in sum, because raised bodies are better than present bodies. To support this overarching argument, v. 45 draws on Genesis 2:7 by a direct quotation introduced with the claim "it is written" (1 Cor. 15:45).[65]

The quotation exactly matches Genesis 2:7 in the Göttingen text, except that Paul describes the person spoken about as "the *first* human" and clarifies that his name is "Adam" (1 Cor. 15:45). Symmachus and Theodotion also include the name "Adam" (ὁ Ἀδὰμ ἄνθρωπος), but in a slightly different order from Paul (ὁ . . . ἄνθρωπος Ἀδὰμ; 1 Cor. 15:45).[66] Consequently, it is unlikely that the inclusion of both "Adam" and "human" originated with Paul.

[64] Contra Thiselton, *First Epistle to the Corinthians*, 1261.
[65] Stark, *Sacred Texts and Paradigmatic Revolutions*, 48.
[66] Hanhart et al., *Septuaginta*, Gen. 2:7.

Rather, this duplication probably reflects Paul's awareness of either a Genesis text or a contemporary interpretation of Genesis that already included the double rendering.[67] In theory, the shift in order could derive from Paul. But one can hardly say whether it does with any certainty, especially if Paul's appeal is to a way of reading Genesis 2:7 rather than a particular way of wording that text.

By contrast, the reference to Adam as "the *first* human" probably does derive from Paul's desire to differentiate between "the first human, Adam, [who] became a living soul" and "the last Adam" who became "a spirit that makes alive" (1 Cor. 15:45).[68] Paul interprets the description of Adam as a "soul" (ψυχή) as being "soulishly animated" (ψυχικός; 1 Cor. 15:46) or "from the earth" and "earthy" (1 Cor. 15:57). By contrast, the last Adam's being a "spirit" (πνεύμα) means his being "spiritually animated" (πνευματικός; 1 Cor. 15:46) and "from heaven" (1 Cor. 15:47; cf. 1 Cor. 2:14–15).

Paul does not make this contrast to highlight the difference between material and immaterial bodies.[69] His point is to highlight the difference between corruptible and incorruptible, or mortal and immortal bodies, and how "just as we have born the image of the earthy person, we also will bear the image of the heavenly person" (1 Cor. 15:49–53).[70] And this difference is not solely in these bodies' duration but also in their quality of existence.[71] Thus the figural relationship between Adam and the Messiah entails both similarities and dissimilarities. On the one hand, they are both humans who inaugurate kinds of human existence. On the other, these kinds of existence are fundamentally

[67] Stanley, *Paul and the Language of Scripture*, 208–9; Thiselton, *First Epistle to the Corinthians*, 1281.

[68] Stanley, *Paul and the Language of Scripture*, 208; Thiselton, *First Epistle to the Corinthians*, 1283.

[69] Thiselton, *First Epistle to the Corinthians*, 1276–77, 1279, 1307, 1309.

[70] Thiselton, *First Epistle to the Corinthians*, 1295.

[71] Thiselton, *First Epistle to the Corinthians*, 1271–72, 1277.

different. Both are embodied, but they are animated by different powers—one earthly and decaying, one heavenly and flourishing.[72] The Messiah's followers are not simply to receive new life, but the Messiah will make them alive with the kind of life that he himself has.

The claim that "the Messiah . . . was raised" necessarily entails his being raised in some way. And the Messiah's resurrection and that of his followers are deeply integrated. Therefore, Paul argues that faithful adherence to the claim of the Messiah's resurrection logically requires the acceptance of a certain view about the nature of the resurrection that the Corinthians should anticipate for themselves.

Spectrum 3: A Future Resurrection with What Outcomes for the Present? (Isa. 25:8 and Hosea 13:14 in 1 Cor. 15:54–55)

In vv. 54–55, Paul concludes his reflections on the transition from bodily corruptibility and mortality to bodily incorruptibility and immortality. The Messiah's followers will experience this transition in the resurrection. Simultaneous with this, Paul claims that the testimony of Isaiah 25:8 and Hosea 13:14 will be fulfilled ("then the word will come to pass").

These prophetic witnesses Paul directly quotes as a single "word."[73] In the case of Isaiah 25:8, Paul's quotation is identical to the text of Isaiah 25:8 attested by Theodotion (θ′): "death has been swallowed up in victory" (1 Cor. 15:54).[74] Contrastingly, Paul's quotation of Hosea 13:14 corresponds to no single known Greek

---

[72] Thiselton, *First Epistle to the Corinthians*, 1284, 1286–88, 1292, 1296–97.

[73] Stark, *Sacred Texts and Paradigmatic Revolutions*, 48.

[74] Hanhart et al., *Septuaginta*, Isa. 25:8; see also Natalio Fernández Marcos, *The Septuagint in Context: Introduction to the Greek Version of the Bible*, trans. Wilfred G. E. Watson (Leiden: Brill, 2000), 142–543; Stanley, *Paul and the Language of Scripture*, 210–11; Florian Wilk, "Isaiah in 1 and 2 Corinthians," in *Isaiah in the New Testament*, ed. Steve Moyise and M. J. J. Menken (New York: T&T Clark, 2005), 146–47.

version, nor does the quotation clearly reflect independent, direct translation from a Hebrew text like the Masoretic. Thus it is not clear precisely which text of Hosea 13:14 Paul might have been using when he quotes it as saying, "Where, Death, is your victory? Where, Death, is your sting?" (1 Cor. 15:55).[75]

By comparison with the Göttingen text, however, Paul's reading might be explained by accommodation to his version of Isaiah 25:8 and some other minor stylistic adjustments. The accommodations to Isaiah 25:8 would involve the exchange of "judgment" (Hosea 13:14) for "victory" (Isa. 25:8 θ′; 1 Cor. 15:55a) and the exchange of "Hades" (Hosea 13:14) for "Death" (Isa. 25:8 θ′; 1 Cor. 15:55b). Some Greek witnesses to Hosea 13:14 have "victory" as Paul does (νῖκος) but in a different form (νίκη).[76] Thus, even if Paul's text of Hosea read with these witnesses, he apparently would still have adjusted his quotation of Hosea to reflect his text of Isaiah because of the form he chooses for this word. The minor stylistic adjustments would then involve pushing back both "victory" and "sting" until after the direct address in each clause.

Following this combined quotation, Paul gives the interpretation that "the sting of death is sin, and the power of sin is the Torah" (1 Cor. 15:56).[77] This interpretation has often been understood as a place where Paul reflects negatively on Israel's legal tradition. More contextually sensitive exegesis, however, shows this is not the case. That "the sting of death is sin" presumably means that death has the power to harm because of sin (cf. Rev. 9:10). And the reason sin has this power to harm by means of death is not that the Torah provokes sinful behavior but precisely that the Torah

---

[75] See Stanley, *Paul and the Language of Scripture*, 211–15.

[76] Hanhart et al., *Septuaginta*, Hosea 13:14.

[77] Only very rarely is it arguable that Paul discusses Greco-Roman "law" or "law" in the abstract. And there is no indication here that Paul has in view anything other than the law given to Israel through Moses. Therefore, I translate νόμος here as "Torah" in order to stress how 1 Cor. 15:56 appeals to Israel's Scriptures.

decrees punishment, including death, for disobedience to the covenant's stipulations (e.g., Deut. 27:9–26, 28:15–68; Lev. 26:14–46).[78]

But "when this corruptible body should be clothed with incorruption and this mortal body should be clothed with immortality" (1 Cor. 15:54a), then death's sting and victory are nullified. "Through [the] Lord Messiah Jesus," this victory is handed over to his followers (1 Cor. 15:57). The implication is that those who have been thus clothed with incorruption and immortality do not sin and so do not activate for sin the power that the Torah gives it to produce death.

Like the Messiah, the bodies of his followers will not be "soulishly motivated" but "spiritually motivated" (1 Cor. 15:44–46; cf. Lev. 23:9–14; Deut. 26:1–19; Prov. 3:9–10; 1 Cor. 15:20, 23, 36–49).[79] In Adam, death spread abroad through sin, but in the Messiah, life immortal and incorruptible spreads abroad to Jesus's followers (1 Cor. 15:21–22, 57; cf. Rom. 5:12–19). This life spreads abroad through the Messiah's gracious gift (1 Cor. 15:57), but it spreads abroad precisely to those who are his *followers*, who do not rest on grace as if it performed its work automatically (*opus operatum*) but who find in grace a renewed summons to follow the Messiah to whose resurrection they have pledged loyalty.[80] Thus accepting Paul's explanation of a future bodily resurrection requires that the Corinthians should presently "be steadfast, immovable, always abounding in the Lord's work because [they] know that [their] labor is not vain in the Lord" (1 Cor. 15:58). The Corinthians' acceptance that "the Messiah . . . was raised" commits them to back this acceptance by lives consistent with and straining forward

---

[78] Cf. Thiselton, *First Epistle to the Corinthians*, 1300–302.

[79] This language is likely an oblique reference to the Holy Spirit (cf. 1 Cor. 2:6–16). See Thiselton, *First Epistle to the Corinthians*, 1175, 1269, 1275, 1277–79, 1286–88, 1292, 1310.

[80] Cf. Dietrich Bonhoeffer, *The Cost of Discipleship*, ed. Irmgard Booth, trans. R. H. Fuller, rev. ed. (New York: Macmillan, 1963), 55–57; Thiselton, *First Epistle to the Corinthians*, 1176.

to the Messiah's immortal and incorruptible life in which they will share.[81]

Conclusion

A "dispositional account of belief" helps highlight that first-person belief does not simply entail acts of asserting specific propositions. Nor is this belief separate from the field of commitments it establishes for other beliefs, behaviors, habits, and practices. Reading 1 Corinthians 15 through this lens stresses the significance of Paul's summary of the early Jesus movement's proclamation in vv. 3b–5. The setting of this summary in vv. 1–11 emphasizes the commitment to this proclamation that Paul and the Corinthians already share. Paul then uses this commitment—especially to the claim that "the Messiah . . . was raised"—as a hermeneutic lever when calling the Corinthians to account for failing to recognize and adhere to this commitment's implications, or to provide it the required "backing" (1 Cor. 15:36).

According to Paul, this backing comes in several forms. First, the Corinthians must accept the Messiah not simply as one who was himself made alive but as one who will also make alive his followers. Second, the Messiah's resurrection entails his session in power and dominion, even over death itself. Third, given these factors, the Messiah's followers should be willing to risk danger, endure difficulty, and persevere in upright behavior consistent with the life to be provided to them by the Messiah in the resurrection. And fourth, this life provided to the followers will be the same kind as experienced by the Messiah himself—embodied existence that moves beyond the constraints of corruptibility and mortality.

Throughout 1 Corinthians 15, these dispositions regularly refract the testimony of Israel's Scriptures. They do so by situating

[81] Thiselton, *First Epistle to the Corinthians*, 1302.

the Messiah as prophetically addressed in the Psalms. Into the deleterious advice to "eat and drink" in Isaiah 22, these dispositions inscribe the actions of those who behave contrary to what the proclamation of the early Jesus movement requires. Such dispositions figure "the first . . . Adam" as both resembling and diverging from "the last Adam." Like "the first . . . Adam," the Messiah inaugurates a particular way of being human. But the description that "the first . . . Adam" became "a living soul" is no longer simply a statement that this "first . . . Adam" ceased being an inanimate bit of molded earth. To be "a living soul" is too limited a scope for the actions of a Messiah who renders death powerless. Thus he is not merely "living" but one who "makes alive." The kinds of life involved are also of wholly different orders—corruptible and conquerable on the one hand, and incorruptible and immortal on the other. Such incorruptibility and immortality imply that the removal of death's "victory" is simultaneously the delivering over of this "victory" into the hands of those who follow the victorious Messiah.

In the end, the New Testament does contain (proto-)creedal formulations, one of which occurs in 1 Corinthians 15:3b–5.[82] Excavating these formulations is critically important to understanding and practicing New Testament theology. But the task cannot stop there. It must move on to contemplating the additional implications of these formulations. Failure to take this additional step runs the risk of translating the New Testament's own polychromatic tradition into, at worst, a polychromatic negative and, at best, a dull monochrome. And, indeed, if we take this task seriously, we may well find that there is not a sharp separation between the New Testament and the earliest Christian theology

[82] See, for example, Bates, *Hermeneutics of the Apostolic Proclamation*, 59–79; J. N. D. Kelly, *Early Christian Creeds*, 3rd ed. (Longman, 1972; repr., London: Continuum, 2011), 16–17; Thiselton, *First Epistle to the Corinthians*, 1186–87.

after it.[83] We may find instead that the dispositional implications within New Testament theology organically and identifiably feed further Christian theological reflection in the coming centuries.

[83] Thiselton, *Hermeneutics of Doctrine*, 42.

3

Ecclesial Unity, Biblical Interpretation, and the Rule of Faith

Keith D. Stanglin

From the 1520s, Protestant history is a story of disagreements over things like baptism, the Lord's Supper, liturgy, free will and predestination, the relationship of the church with civil government, and biblical interpretation, which in many cases was the source of the disagreements. These initial breaks were only the beginning, though. Once Pandora's box was opened, once the precedent was set that any doctrinal disagreement could justify starting a new church, the horrific *possibility* of schism that was realized in the sixteenth century evolved into the accepted *habit* of schism in the seventeenth and eighteenth centuries.[1]

[1]This essay is adapted from Keith D. Stanglin, "The Restoration Movement, the Habit of Schism, and a Proposal for Unity," *Christian Studies* 28 (2016): 7–20, and Keith D. Stanglin, "The Rule of Faith as Hermeneutic," *Christian Studies* 31 (2019): 7–15.

Thomas Campbell's Call for Unity

This habit of schism, transferred from the Old World, became compulsive in the New World. In American soil, nourished by autonomous freedom from old traditions and by optimistic visions of finally making the church what it was supposed to be, the seeds of schism proliferated and flourished. Implicated in this guilt were, among many others, the Presbyterians, whose "Westminster Confession of Faith" and "Westminster Catechism" served as confessional standards and became new sources of conflict.

Many Presbyterians, such as Thomas Campbell, his son Alexander Campbell, and Barton W. Stone, were fed up with the divisive spirit. This frustration is evident in Thomas Campbell's "Declaration and Address" (1809), a sort of manifesto for unity in the church. Campbell insists "that division among christians is a horrid evil, fraught with many evils."[2] As an antidote to the sin of division, Campbell's "Declaration and Address" promotes two fundamental values: (1) the unity of Christians and (2) restoration based on the sole authority of Scripture. He writes:

> To cease from all [divisions], by simply returning to the original standard of christianity—the profession and practice of the primitive church, as expressly exhibited upon the sacred page of New Testament scripture, is the only possible way, that we can perceive, to get rid of those evils. And we humbly think that a uniform agreement in *that* for the preservation of charity would be infinitely preferable to our contentions and divisions: nay, that such a uniformity is the very thing that

---

[2]Thomas Campbell, "Declaration and Address," in *The Quest for Christian Unity, Peace, and Purity in Thomas Campbell's* Declaration and Address: *Text and Studies*, ed. Thomas H. Olbricht and Hans Rollmann (Lanham, MD: Scarecrow, 2000), 19–20. Campbell consistently puts "christian" and "christianity" in lowercase. This typography has been retained throughout this chapter where it appears in quotations.

> the Lord requires, if the New Testament be a perfect model—a sufficient formula for the worship discipline and government of the christian church. Let *us* do, as we are there expressly told *they* did, say as *they* said: that is, profess and practise as therein expressly enjoined by precept and precedent, in every possible instance, after *their* approved example; and in so doing we shall realize, and exhibit, all that unity and uniformity, that the primitive church possessed, or that the law of Christ requires.[3]

It is important to understand the priority and relationship of these two fundamental values. Campbell designates division as the "horrid evil, fraught with many evils," so the unity of God's people is the *end*, the telos, the goal. Restoration, returning to the "profession and practice of the primitive church," is the "only possible way, that we can perceive, to get rid of those evils" of division. In other words, this restoration of faith and practice is the *means*, or the way, to the goal of unity. For Campbell, this vision of patternistic restoration—doing and saying as the New Testament church did and said—based on Scripture alone is the means to the greater goal of unity. Campbell's goal of unity and his means to achieve it do not exclude the possibility of greater, more ultimate ends, such as global evangelism, the praise of God's glory, and so on, for which unity then becomes the means. Rather, we are only observing Campbell's claim that unity is a higher goal than restorationism.[4]

Around the turn of the nineteenth century, the Campbells and other like-minded Reformers initiated what is now known as the American Restoration Movement, envisioned primarily

---

[3] Campbell, "Declaration and Address," 37; italics original.

[4] In fact, there are many ends, some more ultimate than others. For Campbell, unity is a goal that itself becomes a means for more effective evangelism. As for Augustine, the ultimate telos to be enjoyed is God.

as a unity movement within Protestant Christianity. The following years and decades proved that people were less willing than Thomas Campbell anticipated to renounce their denominational creeds and practices that were "not as old as the New Testament."[5] Though not officially or structurally a denomination, the Restoration Movement became, by a loose sociological definition, a distinct denomination.[6] The further, tragic irony is that this same group, a unity movement, experienced its own divisions. In addition to the doctrinal and social reasons for the eventual divisions, later divisions reflected an ideological tension laid out in Campbell's original vision. Unity and restoration, as an enduring pair of principles in the subsequent Restoration Movement, came into tension with one another. This conflict between the two values hinged on the inevitability of differing interpretations of Scripture. On occasions when there was disagreement on the interpretation of Scripture, which value—unity or restoration—would be emphasized in the tension? One stream of the Restoration Movement tended to sacrifice agreement on Scripture

---

[5] Campbell, "Declaration and Address," 19. Alexander Campbell also used similar language: "I commenced my career in this country under the conviction that nothing that was not as old as the New Testament should be made an article of faith, a rule of practice, or a term of communion amongst Christians." "Address to the Public," *Christian Baptist* 2 (1824): 40.

[6] "A denomination is an association or fellowship of congregations within a religion that have the same beliefs or creed, engage in similar practices and cooperate with each other to develop and maintain shared enterprises." D. O. Moberg, "Denominationalism," in *Dictionary of Christianity in America*, ed. Daniel G. Reid (Downers Grove, IL: InterVarsity Press, 1990), 350. This standard definition, which fits mainstream Churches of Christ, would seem to differ from the more formal and overtly ecumenical aspects of a denomination assumed, for example, by Barry Ensign-George, "Denomination as Ecclesiological Category: Sketching an Assessment," in *Denomination: Assessing an Ecclesiological Category*, ed. Paul M. Collins and Barry Ensign-George (New York: T&T Clark, 2011), 1–21. The idea, assumed by Ensign-George, that denominationalism is ecumenically friendly was certainly not the assumption of Campbell, who saw denominational reality as the corollary and culprit of continual division.

for the sake of unity, whereas another stream tended to sacrifice wider unity for a particular interpretation of Scripture. Among the former (represented especially by Disciples of Christ), doctrinal distinctions were easily overlooked and de-emphasized in the practice of open fellowship. Among the latter (represented especially by Churches of Christ), the goal of broader unity was largely effaced by the defense of certain exegetical conclusions.[7]

In a fascinating passage, Campbell left room in his treatise for another, better way. After laying out his plan for achieving unity through restoration—that we should do and say as the first-century church did and said—Campbell immediately writes, "But if after all, our brethren can point out *a better way* to regain and preserve that christian unity and charity expressly enjoined upon the church of God, we shall thank them for the discovery, and cheerfully embrace it."[8] This comment indicates, first, the humility of Campbell in defining his vision for unity. The assertion of openness to further instruction in the search for truth, although formulaic, does not seem to be insincere or rhetorical but rather to communicate a sincere and commendable openness. Second, Campbell's remark shows explicitly which value he considers as the end and which value is the means. Unity is the *conditio sine qua non* "expressly enjoined upon the church of God." The restoration of first-century practices is a means to that unity and not expressly enjoined on the church. Third, Campbell regards the means, which in this case is patternistic restoration, to be potentially dispensable. By "dispensable," I do not mean

[7] Though the dialectic was usually not held in tension successfully, it is an exaggeration to say that unity and restoration are two "mutually exclusive" or "incompatible" goals. For example, Richard T. Hughes, *Reviving the Ancient Faith: The Story of Churches of Christ in America* (Grand Rapids: Eerdmans, 1996; repr., Abilene, TX: Abilene Christian University Press, 2008), 22; M. Eugene Boring, *Disciples and the Bible: A History of Disciples Biblical Interpretation in North America* (St. Louis: Chalice Press, 1997), 112.

[8] Campbell, "Declaration and Address," 37; italics added.

unimportant. Restoration is, to Campbell's mind, the most effective way, "the only possible way, that [he] can perceive," to achieve unity. He leaves the door open, however, in case there is, in his words, "a better way." We can only take him at his word that he is open to a better way toward unity than the program of simplistic restorationism.

Given the history of sectarianism and further division within the Restoration Movement, it should be safe to say that restoration has not been a perfect means to unity. Not only has it actually failed to achieve and maintain unity, but restoration, as described by Campbell, is practically untenable. To be fair, one's hermeneutical practice is often better than one's hermeneutical theory. This seems to have been the case with Campbell. In addition, there have been restorationist hermeneutical proposals sympathetic with Campbell's that provide more nuance regarding which commands and examples are to be followed and how. But by and large, because they use the same approach, such attempts still fail to achieve the desired unity, and they usually fail to relieve people of the abiding impression that sound biblical application is equivalent to imitating, as closely as possible, first-century speech and practice.

Toward a "Better Way" to Unity

If Campbell could see us now, he might be inclined to return to his statement and ask, "Is there 'a better way'?" Regarding Campbell's two fundamental values, where are Churches of Christ now? In attempting to make a long and complex description shorter, I offer the following brief synopsis. Churches of Christ are increasingly diverse, but they still reflect to some degree the tension between restoration and unity. Many congregations still hold to the restoration principle of doing and saying what the first-century church did and said. Most of these congregations have given up on the prospect of broader Christian unity on the basis of this principle and its practice.

Other Churches of Christ have gradually neglected or outright rejected the ideal of patternistic restoration in their embrace of the call to ecumenical unity. Such congregations tend to proceed toward this goal by engaging first with evangelical and other conservative Protestant groups, a natural and commendable move. One concern, though, is that many who have rejected the simplistic sort of restorationism have not really decided what, if anything, to put in its place.

For those who are moved by Campbell's and Christ's calls to unity, is there an alternative to the simplistic restorationist hermeneutic? Can there be one that does not involve being absorbed into another denominational or evangelical identity? Is there, to use Campbell's words, "a better way"?

This better way, in order to achieve real unity among Churches of Christ and beyond, must address the problem of individualistic biblical interpretation that makes each interpreter his own pope. Such an approach has led to divisions as numerous and insidious as those caused by any creed or confession. The better way, while keeping Scripture primary, must provide a lens or an aid in interpretation that guides and limits interpretation.

The better way must also address the "flattening" of Scripture that makes each commandment and article of faith as important as the next. The patternistic restorationism of "doing what they did" has sometimes resulted in an unhealthy equalizing of commands and examples, as well as making possible inferences the equivalent of express commands. By this principle, for instance, the correct frequency of communion became as necessary as practicing it at all. A cappella singing could be considered as central a tenet of the faith as the divinity of Christ. Such thinking led to lists of the necessary articles of faith that could be lengthy and, again, based on one's own individual interpretation of Scripture. Although no true articles of faith are unimportant, the better way must provide a means to distinguish between central and peripheral articles of the faith, thus enabling the church to find and maintain unity in its core beliefs and practices.

If anyone doubts that some doctrines and commands are more important than others, see, for starters, Hosea 6:6; Matthew 7:12, 22:35–40, 23:23; Mark 12:28–34; and 1 Corinthians 15:3–8. To acknowledge that there are "weightier matters of the law" implies that there are also less weighty matters; it does not, however, imply that the less weighty matters should be neglected (Matt. 23:23). But to deny that there are such weightier matters would be to deny the clear meaning of these cited passages.

The Common Content

In the search for this desired but elusive unity, one could take a page from the restorationist playbook and ask the following crucial question about the first-century church: "What is it that united the early church, to the degree that those Christians were united?" Whatever it was, it was not the principle of "Scripture alone." What brought people to Christ and kept them united in him was their common belief in the content of the apostolic proclamation. The content of this faith was passed on publicly in the reading and preaching of the word in early Christian assemblies. Such knowledge was available to a person before and after baptism. It was precisely at baptism, however—which was done in the name of the Father, the Son, and the Holy Spirit—when a person confessed what is central to Christian faith: belief in God the Father, the Son, and the Holy Spirit.[9]

---

[9]The clearest early exposition of these three points is in Irenaeus, *On the Apostolic Preaching* 6, trans. John Behr (Crestwood, NY: St. Vladimir's Seminary Press, 1997), 43–44. One of the best brief summaries of this content is in Frances M. Young, *The Making of the Creeds*, new ed. (London: SCM Press, 2002).

This threefold expression of belief, passed down and received leading up to and at baptism, is what Irenaeus, Tertullian, and other early Christian writers referred to as the "rule of faith," or the "rule of truth," the oral proclamation of the Christian faith handed down from the apostles. It is the measure (*canon*) of the essential truths of Christian faith. Because it was handed down orally, the rule of faith (*regula fidei*) varied somewhat in its exact wording. Despite the verbal variation, there is remarkable consistency in what is said and believed about Father, Son, and Spirit. This increasingly consistent wording reflected the substance of what was confessed periodically at baptism, and a standardized text became a regular part of the church's confession in worship. Eventually, the wording would be transcribed and codified as a creed—that is, a statement of belief. ("Credo," from which "creed" comes, simply means "I believe" and is the initial Latin word in ancient statements of faith.) The rule of faith and ancient creeds, such as the Apostles' Creed, are simply reiterations or extensions of the baptismal confession of faith, which itself is a summary of what the apostles preached.[10] It is no accident, then, that every article of the Apostles' Creed can be tied—and most of them verbatim—to passages in the book of Acts, which records the apostles' preaching.[11] The rule of faith and the creed (the Apostles'

---

[10] For a discussion of this distinction, as well as a fine overview of the rule of faith and its functions, see Everett Ferguson, *The Rule of Faith: A Guide* (Eugene, OR: Cascade, 2015). For slightly more on the Apostles' Creed, see Keith D. Stanglin, "Apostles' Creed," in *Global Dictionary of Theology*, ed. William A. Dyrness and Veli-Matti Kärkkäinen (Downers Grove, IL: InterVarsity Press Academic, 2008), 59–60.

[11] One must supplement with the Gospels according to Matthew and Luke to see that Mary was a "virgin," and the idea that the church is "catholic" (or universal) is implied, but not explicit, in Acts. Alexander Campbell called the Apostles' Creed "a *bonafide* creed; and in every word true." "Campbellism Examined," *Millennial Harbinger* 4, no. 5 (1855): 74; see also William Tabbernee, "Alexander Campbell and the Apostolic Tradition," in *The Free Church and the Early Church: Bridging the Historical and Theological Divide*, ed. D. H. Williams (Grand Rapids: Eerdmans, 2002), 163–80; John Mark Hicks, "Theological

or otherwise) are not the same thing, but they differ more in function than in content. And it is the content with which we are concerned here, so I use the terms more or less interchangeably.

What united the early church was the common confession of apostolic faith. The content of this faith is most easily accessible and summed up in the Apostles' Creed. If one's faith in the basic content of this creed was enough to unite the early church in the face of threats from within and without, then it is also worth considering whether it might provide a "better way" than the isolated biblicism that has failed to unite. How might that way look, or even be justified, in Churches of Christ?

The Value of a Common Confession

First, the better way begins with appreciating the significance of the baptismal confession in Churches of Christ. What is confessed by the one being baptized, which has sometimes been Christocentric rather than Trinitarian, reflects what is regarded as the most important doctrine of the faith. That is, in Churches of Christ, since there is already a tacit acknowledgment that this confession is a statement of belief acceptable for fellowship, there is already a mechanism in place for a common, uniting confession. More, not less, attention should thus be given to a consistent form of confession that is Trinitarian, like baptism itself.

Second, if faith in God the Father, the Son, and the Holy Spirit, as expressed in the Apostles' Creed, is sufficient for full union with

---

Orientation for Churches of Christ: Resourcing Alexander Campbell's Trinitarian *Christian System*," *Christian Studies* 28 (2016): 21–36. Thomas Campbell was also not opposed to creeds per se. Campbell, "Declaration and Address," 26–27, says: "As to creeds and confessions, although we may appear to our brethren to oppose them, yet this is to be understood only in *so far* as they oppose the unity of the church, by containing sentiments not expressly revealed in the word of God; or, by the way of using them, become the instruments of a human or implicit faith: or, oppress the weak of Gods [*sic*] heritage: where they are liable to none of those objections, we have nothing against them. It is the *abuse* and not the *lawful use* of such compilations that we oppose" (italics original).

the body of Christ at baptism, there is no clear reason it cannot be an effective form of unity in the ongoing life of the church. As such, the Apostles' Creed, or something very much like it, should be a regular part of the church's worship, as well as new members' and children's catechesis. For purposes of unity, the faith confessed at baptism should be a sufficient test of fellowship. Such a standard will be easier to maintain if the first suggestion provided here is followed and due attention to the fullness of justifying faith is given at the point of entry. As a result of uniting around a common confession, it would at least make it more difficult for a church to divide or to break fellowship with other churches over tertiary concerns.

Appreciating the significance of baptism and baptismal confession should be easy within Churches of Christ. The use of the rule of faith or a creed, however, could raise some concerns and even objections, some of which could be related to the extreme allergy restorationists have traditionally had to the word "creed." Yet the proposal here is not simply to impose a creed. The point is to recommend the core doctrines that are reflected in the rule of faith and Apostles' Creed, but without imposing any one particular creed or text. But if a creed is chosen for recitation, the Apostles' Creed is a good place to start. It is by no means the only option, but there are advantages to its use in a restorationist setting. It is the most benign, least controversial of early Christian creeds. Campbell and others saw the anathemas and divisions native to the Nicene and Chalcedonian councils, but foreign to the Apostles' Creed, as poisonous to a movement seeking Christian unity. But the language of the Apostles' Creed is biblical, and it was approved by Alexander Campbell himself.[12] In contrast, the Nicene Creed uses an unbiblical word with a shady past

[12] For related bibliography and comments, see note 11 in this chapter.

(*homoousios*), with which no one was overly excited; this word was repeated and extended at Chalcedon (451).

At any rate, the point here does not depend on using the Apostles' Creed specifically, but on uniting around and confessing the faith it reflects. The Apostles' Creed, on its own, is incomplete. It is not an exhaustive summary of the faith and practice of the early church. Its content is one of many canons or rules that regulate that faith and practice. It is used alongside Scripture and liturgy; it does not replace them but coheres with them. If it is faulted for omitting explicit quotations from the Old Testament, then the church should read Scripture, recite the psalms and the Magnificat, all of which provide the context. The opening line of the Apostles' Creed assumes Old Testament teaching and implies something that many Greco-Roman pagans would contest—namely, that God is the efficient cause of the universe, which he created ex nihilo. Moreover, although the rule of faith does not include moral instruction, such instruction and obedience were assumed by anyone who would be united to this faith in baptism. A catechumen who said, "I think abortion is permissible," would not have been baptized.

Can a creed function as a form of unity? Would it actually unite people in their faith? What about those who do not share the faith expressed in the words recited? Of course, people can read into a creed almost anything that they want. This is why the Nicene fathers added the word *homoousios* (a nonbiblical word that the Arians would not affirm) and appended specific anathemas to the creed—namely, because Arians could still confess almost every other word of it, despite the authors' intentions. If this is a problem for the creed, though, it is also a problem for Scripture, which can be used and has been used, to prove just about anything. The content of the rule of faith is fairly straightforward, and it is possible to come to a common understanding of its chief points.

But will reciting a creed every week with the church be adequate to promote unity? Is the content of the creed an effective form of unity for the life of the church? Without providing a formal argument, but based on experience, I can only assert that reciting the same faithful words each week in unison, a common confession of what we and the communion of saints have believed, does promote unity. Is it adequate or sufficient on its own? Perhaps it would be better to think of it as a "starting point." By itself, an isolated recitation of a few words by isolated individuals who know and seek nothing beyond these few words is probably not sufficient. But if discipleship is taken seriously, then these words and their recitation at baptism and every Lord's Day will come to mean more in their biblical, liturgical, moral, and communal contexts than the sum of their parts. Any community's statement of faith acquires its meaning in a worshiping, living, learning community. As stated previously, the rule of faith must not be removed from the context of teaching, practice, and worship. The content of the rule of faith is the stuff of family devotionals, catechesis, and liturgy, embodied in baptism and Eucharist.

What kind of unity and fellowship are we talking about, and is it just a utopian dream? The unity I envision is different than that of Thomas Campbell, who wanted no confessional boundaries. It may be true that his vision was more ambitious and that mine may still allow for denominations. So let me note some things about the unity I have in mind.

What Unity Might Mean

First, unity does not mean total uniformity without distinctions or disagreements. Some degree of disunity is probably inevitable and should not necessarily undermine the unity of spirits in the bond of peace. We already have inter- and intracongregational unity without uniformity of belief and practice. As Origen admitted, any serious school of philosophy will lend itself to sharp disagreements and differences.[13] That is, some degree of division may be inevitable, as long as we see in a glass darkly.

Second, unity does not necessarily mean worshiping every week under the same roof. For instance, we would all admit regional separation. What about ethnic or subcultural preferences? Romans 16:4 speaks of the "churches of the Gentiles" (ESV), implying there are churches of the Jews who presumably enjoy the right hand of fellowship.

Third, the unity I envision opens the door to increased interaction, cooperation, and conversation with other groups—something not historically characteristic of Churches of Christ. Such interaction could lead to even greater unity of faith and practice. We see what we can learn from each other. We may teach others a more biblical view of baptism. We may learn a more thoughtful approach to worship. Such mutual benefit is difficult to achieve in isolation.

In short, unity means a mutual recognition of denominational bodies, congregations, and individuals. There may be levels or degrees of unity. There will always be disagreements, and thus no uniformity. Congregations should still have the right to teach their distinctives and require more for membership. But we should be in conversation with all who call on the name of the Lord Jesus.

Proposals for greater unity are not to be dismissed simply because unity has proven difficult to achieve. To the degree that any proposal for unity causes division, it is worth questioning. As such, Campbell's proposal, whose vision inspired at least three new sects, could be classified among those worth questioning. But since unity is enjoined everywhere in the New Testament, we cannot be dubious of all proposals any more than we can dismiss the New Testament as a relic of the past. Even if it never happens this side of the eschaton, we cannot give up on unity any more

[13] Origen, *Contra Celsum*, §§3.12–13, trans. Henry Chadwick (Cambridge: Cambridge University Press, 1980), 135–36.

than we can give up on the call to perfection (Matt. 5:48), utopian as both may be. But what if *this* proposal for unity is simply an attempt to diagnose the causes of division and suggest a prescription that served the early church reasonably well? What if the prescription has been applied in a number of believing communities with success?

Rule of Faith as Hermeneutic

Another aspect of this proposal is that the rule of faith must come alongside the reading of Scripture. To recognize the importance of the rule of faith in this way is not to undermine the primacy of Scripture for the church. In fact, in this proposal, Scripture is just as central as Campbell imagined.

The aim is not to dispense with Scripture but only with a certain way of reading and applying Scripture. The difference is that the rule functions as a conscious guide and lens for biblical interpretation.[14] The rule of faith is not a sufficient hermeneutical theory or method of interpretation, but it is a necessary supplement to responsible exegesis and application. This suggestion runs counter to the Enlightenment-era idea, shared by most restorationists, that one should read the Bible as if it has never been read before, giving no thought to previous traditions or interpretations. Rather, the rule of faith helps limit biblical interpretation, and its focus on the core of the gospel helps keep inferential interpretations and applications in their proper place.[15]

The rule of faith had many functions in the ante-Nicene church, but we are interested here in how it functioned as a hermeneutical key to Scripture. Before modern exegetes excluded all theological presuppositions from biblical interpretation, an

[14] For example, see Robert W. Jenson, *Canon and Creed*, Interpretation (Louisville: Westminster John Knox Press, 2010).

[15] Thomas Campbell made it clear that inferences should not be binding as tests of fellowship. Campbell, "Declaration and Address," 18–19.

essential feature of biblical exegesis was the insistence on interpreting Scripture within the boundaries set by the rule of faith and the whole of Scripture. Premodern exegetes read Scripture overtly through a theological lens. The reason is simple, and it is as true now as it has always been: *nuda scriptura*—bare Scripture interpreted objectively without the interference of creeds or traditions—does not guard against false teaching.

That *nuda scriptura* is inadequate to the task is evident already in the New Testament. The devil himself knew and quoted Scripture to support his case (Matt. 4:5–6). His was probably an intentional misuse. In 2 Peter 3:16, the writer acknowledges that ignorant and unstable interpreters have twisted the meaning of Paul's letters and other Scriptures. Theirs was more likely an unintentional misuse. In order to counter such possible interpretations by Gnostics in the second century, Irenaeus suggested that Scripture should be interpreted according to the proper *hypothesis*, or principle. The *hypothesis* acts as a pattern or lens through which Scripture is read. Irenaeus invites us to think of Scripture as a mosaic, the pieces of which are intended to form a beautiful image of a majestic king. This is indeed the natural image, which makes sense of all the various pieces. It is possible, however, to arrange the pieces so as to form an image of a hideous animal. The fit is not as natural, but it is possible.[16] The *hypothesis* is the pattern that, like the box of a jigsaw puzzle, confirms the correct image and can even be used on the front end to steer the worker toward the correct image. For Irenaeus, the *hypothesis* that guides readers in the right interpretation of Scripture is the rule of faith.

My contention is that the doctrine contained in the early church's rule of faith and, to a degree, in the later tradition of the church ought to play a role in the church's ongoing interpretation of Scripture not unlike its role in the early church. The rule of faith

[16] Irenaeus, *Against Heresies*, §1.8.1, trans. Dominic J. Unger, Ancient Christian Writers 55 (New York: Newman, 1992), 41.

is not all one needs for exegesis. It never stood alone in the life and teaching of the church, and it does not stand alone in biblical interpretation. It is, however, a minimal requirement. As with the attention given to potential concerns over the use of the rule of faith in its contribution to unity, the remainder of this essay will seek to address some concerns and benefits that may arise from a conscious use of the rule of faith and Christian tradition in the exegetical task. In the process, the hermeneutical role of the rule of faith should become a little clearer.[17]

Concerns

In a Christian fellowship whose foundational identity was forged by its opposition to creeds and confessions of faith on the principle of (as we would put it now) *nuda scriptura*, objections are bound to be raised against the suggestion of inviting an interpretive lens to come alongside Scripture. Let us consider and offer brief responses to three primary concerns.

Objection 1. The first objection may go something like this: "The Bible is the only rule of Christian faith and practice. No interpretive aid should be added to it." But the Bible does not come with its own hermeneutic. It is not self-interpreting, at least not enough to guarantee that truth-seeking readers will not arrive at some wildly different conclusions regarding meaning and application. Given this reality, even restorationists have supplied various hermeneutical aids, all of which are external to Scripture. The principle "no creed but the Bible" is itself an extrabiblical creed. On the popular level, slogans have tended to function as extrabiblical

[17] Scripture and the rule of faith are two distinct sides of the same coin, each informing the other, neither one to be used to the exclusion of the other. For more on Irenaeus and the rule of faith as a hermeneutical guide, see Keith D. Stanglin, *The Letter and Spirit of Biblical Interpretation: From the Early Church to Modern Practice* (Grand Rapids: Baker Academic, 2018), 29–35. Many of the other themes in this article are treated in more detail in this volume as well.

hermeneutical lenses. "Speak where the Bible speaks, and be silent where it is silent" is perhaps the best known of these slogans. On a more scholarly level, leaders have felt the need to advocate and explain various methods and principles. Alexander Campbell has his seven principles of interpretation, and D. R. Dungan his hermeneutics textbook.[18] And who could forget the celebrated threefold hermeneutic of application—express command, approved example, and necessary inference? All these are hermeneutical lenses we have invited to come alongside Scripture.

We may discuss whether this or that hermeneutical lens is more or less consistent with Scripture or seems to be in accord with the evidence in Scripture. But speaking strictly, any hermeneutical lens will be extrabiblical. This acknowledgment alone is no more a strike against the rule of faith than it is against beloved slogans or methods such as command-example-inference. Among the many extrabiblical hermeneutical rules available, the rule of faith has the advantage of historical pedigree. The early church engaged in Scripture reading and application according to the interpretive traditions of Jesus and his apostles.[19]

Objection 2. A second objection may be considered: "If you read the Bible through a lens, then that lens ends up obscuring the view. Objectivity is replaced with subjectivity." Alexander Campbell argued against reading Scripture through the lens of any creed, for interpreters will find in the Bible the content of what they already believe: "If I must examine the Bible through the creed, then the creed is my eyes—my artificial eyes (for it cannot be my natural eyes)—my spectacles. If my spectacles are green glass, the Bible is also green; if blue, the Bible is blue; and as is the creed, so is the

[18] Alexander Campbell, "The Bible—Principles of Interpretation," *Millennial Harbinger* 3, no. 1 (1846): 13–24; D. R. Dungan, *Hermeneutics: A Text-book*, 2nd ed. (Cincinnati: Standard, 1888).

[19] For example, see Luke 24:44–49; Rom. 12:6; 1 Cor. 11:23; 15:3; 2 Thess. 2:15; 3:6.

Bible to me."[20] According to Campbell, presuppositions impede the objectivity that is necessary for discerning the truth. When a reader approaches the Bible through the lens of anything other than the Bible itself, that lens obscures the message of the Bible.

It is a legitimate concern that the lens or window through which the text is viewed becomes the object of viewing, thus obscuring what was the ostensible object. The concern here is that doctrinal presuppositions like those found in the rule of faith or in later creeds impede exegetical objectivity. And to a certain extent, Campbell is right. A green lens indeed makes the Bible appear green, and a blue lens makes it look blue. But what if those doctrinal presuppositions are right? What if the green lens is, in fact, the correct lens? There should then be no problem with it. With the rule of faith, readers have the correct lens, or at least the properly Christian lens. Again, the Bible is not self-interpreting. A lens will be used, and there are incorrect lenses.

As in Irenaeus's analogy of the mosaic, the correct *hypothesis*, like a jigsaw puzzle box top, does cause the artist to see each and every piece through that pattern. Every piece looks like it contributes to the picture of the king. The worker cannot help but be influenced by the pattern and indeed wants to be guided by it. At the same time, however, the lens or pattern does not eliminate all objectivity. One can still take a step back and see how the mosaic fits better with the proper *hypothesis* than it does with any alternative. Those other interpretations, though possible, do not fit as easily with the rest of the picture. One would have to force the pieces together unnaturally to form a picture of someone or something other than the king.

Objection 3. For those who may be sympathetic to the rule of faith and tradition, a third set of questions may still arise: "Whose tradition will we follow, how much authority does it have, and

---

[20] Alexander Campbell, "Reply," *Christian Baptist* 5 (1827): 209.

when does the normative tradition chronologically cease?" My suggestion does not entail an attempt to heed everything that every church has ever said.

A distinction should be made between the ancient rule of faith and later traditions. Of the two, the rule of faith is primary, both logically and chronologically. It represents the earliest Christian consensus on the core teachings about God, Christ, and creation. In later tradition, as in a choir, some voices stand out above the others for their superior quality; other voices may be more or less off-key.[21] This distinction between the earlier and the later tradition, with the preference for the former, is neither arbitrary nor unique to restorationist primtivism. It is ubiquitous throughout church history. The decrees of councils both ancient and modern seek to base their judgments on the earlier tradition. For our purposes, we may point out that the fading of the oral, living memory of Jesus and the apostles signaled the diminishing reliability of the developing oral tradition and coincided with increasing reliance on the written tradition that became canonized as the New Testament. The Roman Church of Trent and the Vatican Councils may claim to be the same institutional church that long ago proclaimed the rule of faith and gave us the creeds and written canon, but the two churches are not essentially the same. It is like asking whether Aaron and Caiaphas shared the same high priesthood—yes and no. These two churches are as different as the dogma of the Assumption of Mary is from the claim of the virginal conception. We are not bound to follow the voices whose tones are dissonant with or wildly different from the original musical score.

Thus the tradition is not infallible, especially regarding matters that are not specified in the rule of faith. A novel interpretation of Scripture that has never been conceived in two millennia could be

---

[21] I am here expanding on the chorus analogy given in Jaroslav Pelikan, *The Christian Tradition: The Emergence of the Catholic Tradition (100–600)* (Chicago: University of Chicago Press, 1971), 122.

correct. Some advances in our knowledge of ancient history, particularly that of the ancient Near East, enhance this possibility. The point, though, is that a biblical interpreter should hear the chorus of voices and have a very good reason for differing with them.

Benefits

If potential concerns over introducing the rule of faith as a hermeneutical key can be satisfactorily answered, is there a positive case to be made for the proposal? For believers who are more or less satisfied with the status quo, what are the benefits of such an approach?

First, reading Scripture with the rule of faith reminds us of our primary identity as Christians. It reminds us that we are to read Scripture not as disinterested scientists but as Christians. There may and should be an attempt at objectivity, but there is no such thing as pure hermeneutical objectivity. As Robert Jenson said, the creed is our "critical theory" of interpretation.[22]

Second, reading with the Christian tradition opens up true interpretive possibilities. The American Restoration Movement began to flourish at the same time that modern exegesis came to dominate, especially in the academy. As a result of this coincidence, some principles of the so-called historical-critical method, particularly the emphasis on human authorial intent, have been taken for granted in the movement. The search for human authorial intent tends to exclude all meanings that could not possibly have crossed the mind of the human author. To be sure, human authorial intent, when it is discernible, should remain the starting point for exegesis, but interpretation should not end there.

Third, reading with the Christian tradition helps limit false interpretations. As noted previously, such regulation of the range of possible interpretations was the only way to ensure Scripture

[22] Jenson, *Canon and Creed*, 81.

would not be used in support of heresy. Timothy George compares this regulation to a guardrail that helps keep travelers on the right path when they find themselves on a dangerous highway.[23]

Fourth, reading Scripture alongside the Christian doctrinal, moral, and liturgical traditions could help bring greater unity to divided churches. The old saying, "In necessary things, unity; in nonnecessary things, liberty; in both, charity," begs the question of what falls in which category. The categories are indisputable. What goes where is not, yet Scripture does provide a few answers. The line may remain somewhat blurry, but tradition is an aid that confirms which doctrines are more central and which are more peripheral.

Finally, to acknowledge the role of the rule of faith and the influence of the Christian theological and exegetical tradition in biblical interpretation is simply to make explicit what is likely already implicit and practiced. In other words, exegetes are, in fact, shaped by the Christian tradition. This is true even of exegetes who deny the influence. Even the most anticreedal, traditionless Christians read Scripture through the lens of received tradition.

A Rule for Restoration

All Christians should have an interest in Christ's prayer that his followers be united. As heirs of a Christian unity movement known more for its divisiveness than its unity, Churches of Christ perhaps have a special obligation to consider the problem within their own ranks and work toward resolution. Thomas Campbell certainly felt the call to promote unity, and to that end, he proposed going back to Scripture alone to restore first-century beliefs and practices.

Interestingly, he did leave room for a "better way" to promote unity, if one could be found. Two centuries of history have shown that the patternistic hermeneutic of restoration that Campbell

[23] Timothy George, *Reading Scripture with the Reformers* (Downers Grove, IL: InterVarsity Press Academic, 2011), 123.

seems to have endorsed has not served the goal of unity as effectively as he envisioned. In light of Campbell's own concession and in the spirit of seeking to restore the unity of the early church, we seek a better way.

The better way is to allow the "great tradition" of the church, the collection of voices from Christian history, in all of their unity and even their multiplicity, to have a seat at the table in the life of the church, including in the church's interpretation and application of Scripture. The unity of this tradition, expressed well in many sources, is succinctly stated in the rule of faith.[24] And as Everett Ferguson writes, the rule of faith "sustains unity in diversity and disagreement."[25]

The proposal here is for "deep restoration." By deep restoration, I mean restoration that is not fixated simply on *what* the first-century church said and did but more on *how* they thought and *why* they said and did thus. Such a perspective will often result in saying and doing as the first-century church, but the saying and doing will go deeper and tap into the fount from which the practices flow. This fount is the gospel, the rule; this is the pattern to be followed. This pattern is revealed in the apostolic proclamation of what God has done for his people in Christ, and it is summed up in the rule of faith and early creeds. This is how the early church thought, and this is how they read the Bible. This proposal should be a welcome possibility for those who have rejected traditional "restorationism" but have yet to find anything to put in its place. It should also be considered by those who have held more firmly to the traditional patternistic way but have been discouraged by the lack of unity that it actually provides.

---

[24] The compatibility of a restoration perspective with an appreciation for church history is discussed in Keith D. Stanglin, "Restorationism and Church History: Strange Bedfellows?" *Christian Studies* 26 (2013–2014): 21–32.

[25] Ferguson, *Rule of Faith*, 84. Ferguson describes many beneficial uses of the rule of faith in today's church. *Rule of Faith*, 83–90.

Opening the door to the broader tradition and history of the church throughout the ages will come with a new set of questions: How much influence should a particular tradition have, and how should a particular tradition exercise influence in an interpretive community? There will be tension, and the voices of tradition often will not solve the question. But they will enhance the conversation. As an analogy, consider the function of case laws in jurisprudence. For any particular case at hand, lawyers have before them a long history and a myriad of cases relevant to the law's interpretation and application, some of which may even be contradictory. Some of these decisions are more precedent-setting than others because of their wisdom, practicality, extensive reach, and ability to stand the test of time and to gather consensus over a long period.[26] Similarly, the church's tradition, though complex, can speak with faithful wisdom to those willing to listen. This extended conversation can enhance the church's current conversations and help unite Christians liturgically, doctrinally, and morally. It is good to acknowledge and welcome the voices of the Christian past into the life of our churches. In them is much wisdom, perspective, and truth to inform our faith, ethics, and liturgy, as well as our biblical interpretation. It is an alternative to *nuda scriptura* in favor of *prima scriptura*. That is, Scripture is the first and primary authority for faith and practice but not necessarily the only voice to be heard.[27]

This proposal assumes, of course, that Christians know both the Scriptures and the ancient tradition of interpretation. Restorationists, who typically have been known for their biblical

---

[26] Giulio Silano provides an extended analogy between a casebook and Peter Lombard's *Sentences*. "Introduction," in Peter Lombard, *The Sentences, Book 1: The Mystery of the Trinity*, trans. Giulio Silano (Toronto: Pontifical Institute of Mediaeval Studies, 2007), xix–xxvi. This seems to be a helpful way to think about the whole Christian tradition.

[27] For more on *nuda scriptura* and *prima scriptura*, see Stanglin, *Letter and Spirit of Biblical Interpretation*, 130–32.

literacy, have often ignored church history and tradition. In other words, their biblical literacy has usually been accompanied by a willful, general Christian illiteracy—that is, ignorance and rejection of the traditions, creeds, doctrines, and influential figures of the church's history, as well as ignorance of the doctrines and practices of the wider contemporary Christian world. More recently, this ignorance of the greater tradition is being addressed in some of these churches. But it is troubling that, as some restorationist churches are perhaps becoming slightly more literate in general Christian faith and tradition, their biblical literacy is sharply declining across the board. Like other fellowships, Churches of Christ are in the midst of an identity crisis. Being anchored in both Scripture and the Christian tradition could help prevent this denominational identity crisis from mutating and becoming simply a Christian identity crisis.

The point of this essay is not to solve all the problems but to start a conversation that is relevant to the future of Churches of Christ in particular and, more generally, Christianity at large. When I consider the past, an appreciation for the rule of faith that is concerned with the deep restoration I propose would arguably have prevented many divisions that we have seen in the Restoration Movement and reduced the antagonism. When I look toward the present and future, I see this proposal as not altogether different from Thomas Campbell's, but for a different time. In other words, for such a time as this, although I think some "Church of Christ distinctives" are important, I am less engaged about anyone's denominational distinctives, and I tend to be more interested in how the church will survive the impending dark ages—or, closer to home, how we can best pass on the faith to the next generation. In that sense, my interest in ecumenical discussion and the identity of Churches of Christ is connected with and perhaps in service to the question of how we may unify with like-minded Christians to pass on the faith, and how we can best do that in Churches of Christ. The irony is that creeds, long identified in the Restoration Movement as the source of division, may instead be a factor that helps unite.

Like Thomas Campbell, we are open to and seek a better way toward Christian unity and maturity. Whatever that way is, it will not succeed if it is simply another method. No method will save us from ourselves. As long as humans are involved and have their way, even the best way can end in division. Rather, the help of the Holy Spirit is needed to grant knowledge, wisdom, perspective, humility, and love, all of which are necessary if Christians are to be one, to the praise of God's glory.

4

Resisting the Primitivist Temptation

Stephen D. Lawson

You are not here to verify,
Instruct yourself, or inform curiosity
Or carry report. You are here to kneel
Where prayer has been valid.
—T. S. Eliot, "Little Gidding"[1]

This essay considers the notion of "primitivism" in Christian history, and here I begin by acknowledging that this term requires some form of explanation.[2] At its most basic level, primitivism names the impulse to correct errors in faith or practice by returning to teachings or practices that precede the decline that caused the errors. Periodically throughout the two millennia since Pentecost, Christians have attempted to diagnose abuses in practice or errors in doctrine as the consequence of an earlier error or

[1]T. S. Eliot, *Collected Poems 1909–1962* (London: Faber, 1974), 201.

[2]I would like to thank the editors for the invitation to be part of this project. I would also like to thank Joshua Fleer for his thoughtful engagement with an earlier draft of this essay.

series of errors. Christians have then prescribed as an antidote the recovery of beliefs or practices that antedate the error or errors. Such a broad definition encompasses not only movements, such as Mennonites or Puritans, who explicitly used the term "primitive" in their self-description. It encompasses countless devotional and reform movements throughout church history, such as the Desert Fathers of the fourth century, the Franciscans of the thirteenth century, or the *devotio moderna* of the late fourteenth century.

The seeming ubiquity of this method of renewal throughout Christian history should not come as a surprise. The biblical witness is replete with calls to recover from the past something helpful for overcoming errors in the present. One of the persistent themes in Scripture, especially the Old Testament, is the call to abandon faithlessness and remember the covenant, return to God, and honor the ancient ways (e.g., Exod. 13:3, 20:8; Deut. 8:2; 2 Kings 22:11–13; 1 Chron. 16:12–18; Jer. 6:16). In the New Testament, there are the calls to remember the first love and hold fast to the gospel as it was first preached (e.g., Gal. 1:6–9; Rev. 2:5).

When understood as a call to question the beliefs and practices of Christians in the present by judging them against ancient norms, this impulse is both good and necessary. If we fail to reflect thoughtfully on the practices of Christianity in the present in light of the ways in which they differ from older forms of Christianity, we are depriving ourselves of one of the most powerful ways of resisting uncritical absorption of cultural habits incompatible with the faith. When we contrast the present practice of Christianity with that of ancient and biblical modes, our eyes can be opened to the ways in which we have unknowingly accepted as natural and inevitable things that are neither—indeed things that are quite recent. To a certain extent, then, the primitivist impulse is an essential part of the way that Christians should appeal to the past.

In modernity, however, this impulse to return of the fount of the faith underwent a substantial transformation. Within the span of a generation, many people went from seeing the world of Jesus and the apostles in continuity with their own world to seeing their connection with it as tragically severed because of an alleged fall of the church into degeneration. For centuries prior to the era of Renaissance and Reformation in western Europe, the earliest Christians and especially Scripture were understood as major sources of spiritual and theological authority. These sources would often be appealed to by those seeking to enrich and renew the faith, but this wellspring of renewal was meditated to the present through an organic continuity of the church in historical time.

The intellectual and theological revolution that shook western Europe in the fifteenth and sixteenth centuries called into question this historical continuity. Some began to see a "pure" Christianity in its nascent forms, a purity that had been tarnished or outright abandoned for centuries by the corruption of sin. This approach to history, properly called *primitivism*, is a novelty of modernity. The novelty lies not in according a special normative significance to a particular past moment. It lies not even in the patternistic claim to discover a blueprint in that past but in the belief that, between the past and the present, there lies an unredeemable abyss of corruption.

This is what I mean by *primitivism* for the remainder of this essay: primitivism as a theology of history. It is my contention that primitivism thus understood is a temptation—one that should be resisted in the church. In what follows, I aim to present some historical and theological reasons why primitivist approaches to the past, including those explicitly and implicitly employed throughout the Stone-Campbell Movement's two-century history, are so dangerous. I begin by situating them in greater detail within the history of humanity's understanding of the past. History is no stable object of inquiry; it is subject to the vicissitudes of time. History has a history, as it were, and it is to that history we must attend.

However, it first seems fitting to consider if there is a distinction between "primitivism" and "restorationism." Richard Hughes has suggested that such a distinction could be made.[3] Such a distinction could help nuance different ways in which the normativity of early Christianity functions in the present. Regardless of what distinctions could be made between them, as approaches to the Christian past, both primitivism and restorationism rely on the same picture of history: one that begins in purity and is followed by a subsequent fall into corruption, which is followed by the recent return to the pristine state of things. It is this approach to history that I address in this essay. This understanding of primitivism has unfortunately pervaded Christianity in modernity, especially (but by no means exclusively) in its Protestant forms. Yet this approach to the past is historically problematic and theologically dangerous.

The Rise of Successionist Christian History

Christianity is an essentially historical faith. It is founded upon events that happened at a particular place and time. Christianity is thus affected by all of the contingencies of humanity's historical existence (language, culture, etc.). The term that seemed most fitting for the earliest Christians to describe the content of their faith was "gospel" (*euangelion*): a message reporting a good occurrence. The particular good occurrence the earliest Christians were most concerned with was that, with the death and resurrection of Jesus, something incredible had happened that changed everything.

The earliest Christians were so confident of the cosmic significance of Easter that they believed it inaugurated the last days. God would swiftly act to bring all of history's discordant happenings to a conclusion, ushering in an eternal and death-less new creation.

[3]Richard T. Hughes, "Introduction: On Recovering the Theme of Recovery," in *The American Quest for the Primitive Church*, ed. Richard T. Hughes (Chicago: University of Illinois Press, 1988), 3.

As the years slipped into decades and eventually centuries, the confidence of the immediacy of Christ's return waned, resulting in a theological crisis in which eschatological immediacy gave way to worldly comfort (e.g., in Christianity becoming the official religion of the Roman Empire). If the center of God's activity in human history is Jesus, then does temporal distance from the historical moment of his resurrection mean a greater distance from God and God's activity with the world? Of course, the answer to this question has to be negative if the faith is going to live up to its claim to be universal good news for all peoples and for all time. But how does this work? It can only be that the events of Jesus's death and resurrection bring about a new reality that persists through human history. Christians call this new reality "church," the Spirit-filled community of those who have been called out of darkness into light (1 Pet. 2:9).

The early Christians understood the church as a dynamic, living reality. Organic images of the church as a body, a family, and so forth pervade the New Testament. But the early Christians also understood the church as a vessel that carried an unchanging truth through time. The church holds on to a "deposit" that has been "received from the Lord" and "handed on" to believers in the present (1 Cor. 11:23, 15:1–5; 1 Tim. 6:20; 2 Tim. 1:13–14).[4] The church is vital, active, and capable of responding to changes. It is also stable, grounded in continuity through time.

The interplay of the vital and stable elements of the church contributed to its explosive growth in late antiquity. Here was a reality in which God's continued activity was not just palpable but palatable. God could be seen, smelled, touched, and tasted in the church's eucharistic worship. Writing in the middle of the second century, Justin Martyr voices the universal consensus of the earliest Christians when he writes of the Eucharist:

[4] Unless otherwise indicated, Scripture translations are the author's.

> We do not receive these things as common bread nor common drink, but *as Jesus Christ* our savior who became incarnate by God's word and took flesh and blood for our salvation, *so also* have we been taught that the food consecrated through the word of prayer that is from him, from which our blood and flesh are nourished by transformation, *is the flesh and blood of that Jesus who became incarnate.*[5]

One could find similar words in the writings of Ignatius, Irenaeus, Origen, or many other early Christian writers. They all testify that Christian worship was above all a celebration of the active presence of the living Christ.[6]

This dynamic and active aspect of the church was maintained by an underlying stability. The church's claim to an apostolic foundation required a continuity of faith and practice across geography and generations. The gospel preached in Rome in AD 100 needed to be the same as that preached in Constantinople in AD 300. For early Christians, claiming that some teaching was original and innovative was not a compliment indicative of creative genius; it was an accusation of heresy.

It was the first great church historian, Eusebius of Caesarea, who attempted to articulate with precision exactly how the church's stability endures through the contingencies of historical time. Eusebius's *Ecclesiastical History* was the first attempt at writing a comprehensive account of the history of the church.[7] He compiled hundreds of sources and stories from across the ancient world.

---

[5] Justin Martyr, *First Apology*, §66; italics added. This translation is based on but slightly altered from Justin Martyr, *The First and Second Apologies*, trans. Leslie William Barnard (New York: Paulist, 1997), 70.

[6] Cf. Robert Louis Wilken, *The Spirit of Early Christian Thought: Seeking the Face of God* (New Haven, CT: Yale University Press, 2003), 25–49.

[7] Eusebius, *The History of the Church from Christ to Constantine*, trans. G. A. Williamson, rev. and ed. Andrew Louth (New York: Penguin, 1989).

While many had attempted to write down accounts of important events or people (e.g., hagiographies, martyrdom accounts), Eusebius set out to tell the whole story. It was essential for him to demonstrate that history is knowable and thus that Jesus Christ is knowable through it. For Eusebius, it was also essential to demonstrate that the proper vessel and interpreter of history is orthodox, catholic Christianity visibly manifested in the church.[8]

Eusebius's history thus served multiple essential functions for the early church. It demonstrated a continuity of faith and doctrine from Jesus's life to Eusebius's present, answering the problem presented by the increasing historical distance from the Easter event. It also answered the difficulties posed by the multiplicity of truth claims. The church of the early fourth century was rife with competing interpretations over the meaning of the event of Jesus Christ, of the texts that claimed to describe that event, and over how best to practice worship and organize the church. Eusebius's history helped answer the question of who was speaking the properly Christian truth. Finally, Eusebius's history helped answer the problem of unfulfilled Christian eschatology. Eusebius interpreted the imminence given to Jesus's return in the New Testament with the rise of a Christian emperor in Rome. On this account, history is in continuity with Jesus Christ, whose gospel is carried through time in the church's faith and practice, as evidenced by God's providential guidance in the victory of Christianity in the wider culture.

Augustine provided a much richer theological foundation for a Christian vision of history marked by continuity in his magisterial *City of God*.[9] Augustine set to work writing this great work after the sack of Rome in 410, an event that felt cataclysmic to

---

[8] Here the terms *orthodox* and *catholic* are used in their basic lexical meaning: *orthodox* means "correct teaching"; *catholic* means "universal."

[9] Augustine of Hippo, *The City of God against the Pagans*, trans. and ed. R. W. Dyson (Cambridge: Cambridge University Press, 1998).

many in the ancient world. Although it had projected military and cultural stability for a millennium, the "eternal city" was shown to be fragile. Given the different context, it makes sense that the tone Augustine adopts in *City of God* starkly contrasts with Eusebius. Eusebius's *Ecclesiastical History* exudes the optimism that followed the first conversion of a Roman emperor. That optimism has been tempered by a deep awareness of the persistence of sin in Augustine's *City of God*, where the city of God and the earthly city are engaged in a continual struggle up until the end of time.

Augustine's protégé, Paulus Orosius, expanded the arguments of the later sections of *The City of God*, marshaling additional historical evidence that it was not the abandonment of the old gods for Christianity that resulted in Rome's demise. With Orosius, we arrive at that model of history that dominated Christianity throughout the medieval period. This history, writes Anthony Kemp, is "an intellectual city, in which everything is present, included within its wall. It is history as a sacrament, a transubstantial act of evocation of the intangible, the past, made tangible to the feeling intellect of faith."[10] This approach to the Christian past, whereby historical truth is mediated to the present through unswerving continuity, could be called successionist.[11] Like a monarchy gives stability to a government by the seamless transition from one king to his heir, this approach to the past claims stability through uninterrupted succession.

It is not difficult to find writings from the medieval period that illustrate this successionist appeal to continuity. In the fifth

---

[10] Anthony Kemp, *The Estrangement of the Past: A Study in the Origins of Modern Historical Consciousness* (Oxford: Oxford University Press, 1991), 33.

[11] For more on the successionist approaches to the Christian past, as well as the supersessive approaches that supplanted them, see Kenneth Parker, "Coming to Terms with the Past: The Role of History in the Spirituality of John Henry Newman," in *Newman and Life in the Spirit: Theological Reflection on Spirituality for Today*, ed. John R. Connolly and Brian Hughes (Minneapolis: Fortress, 2014), 51–74.

century, Vincent of Lérins wrote that "in the Catholic Church itself, all possible care must be taken, that we hold that faith which has been believed everywhere, always, by all. . . . This rule we shall observe if we follow universality, antiquity, consent."[12] The person sitting in the papal throne might change, but the substance of the faith itself remained static, carried through time unaffected by its vicissitudes.

The hesitancy to acknowledge historical change can be seen in the periodic attempt throughout the medieval period to antedate contemporary practices with historical justification. Perhaps the most famous of these attempts was the so-called *Donation of Constantine*, an eighth-century text that purported to be written by the fourth-century emperor Constantine. In the text, Constantine confers jurisdictional primacy over the western empire to the papacy in gratitude for Pope Sylvester's miraculous healing of Constantine's leprosy.

Sometime in the ninth century, the *Donation* was included with other documents in a collection now referred to as the "Pseudo-Isidorian Decretals." There, it served as "a proof-text for the inviolability of ecclesiastical property."[13] It proved to be a valuable resource for the papacy to bolster its claims to temporal power during the investiture controversy in the eleventh century.

The *Donation* was widely accepted as authentic until Lorenzo Valla's fifteenth-century treatise argued that it was a forgery. Even so, most Roman Catholic writers continued to tacitly accept the *Donation* as authentic until the late sixteenth century. Much has been written about the *Donation*—its origin, textual history, and reception. I refer to its history here only to illustrate that it was an

---

[12] Vincent of Lérins, *Commonitory*, §2.6, in *Nicene and Post-Nicene Fathers of the Christian Church, Second Series*, vol. 11, trans. Philip Schaff and Henry Wace (New York: Christian Literature, 1894), 132.

[13] Janet Nelson, "Kingship and Empire," in *The Cambridge History of Medieval Political Thought, c. 350–c. 1450*, ed. J. H. Burns (Cambridge: Cambridge University Press, 1988), 231.

attempt to ground contemporary faith and practice in antiquity, a hallmark of the successionist approach to history that cannot acknowledge any substantial change. When compared to the historical reasoning of later centuries, the contrast is striking.

The Invention of Primitivism

The humanists in the fourteenth and fifteenth centuries (Valla among them) helped prepare for the dethroning of the successionist approach to the past. Originally focused on classical Greek and Roman authors, the Renaissance humanists began to invoke a tripartite approach to history. In the fourteenth century, the Italian writer Petrarch, seen by many as the founder of humanism, appropriated images of light for the distant past and dark for the near past.

Originally, Petrarch used the image of darkness to refer to the time before the coming of Christ and the time after Christ, writing with pity about Cicero, who unfortunately died before Christ—that is, before "the end of darkness and the night of error," before "the dawn of the true light."[14] Over time, as Petrarch helped inaugurate a "rebirth" in art and letters though his devotion to Greek and Roman culture, the metaphor he employed became reversed. Theodore Mommsen writes that men who took up Petrarch's mantel

> contrasted the "rebirth" of the arts and letters which, they held, had been effected by Dante, Giotto, and Petrarch, with the preceding period of cultural darkness. With this change of emphasis from things religious to things secular, the significance of the old metaphor became reversed: Antiquity, so long considered as the

[14] Petrarch, *De sui ipsius et multorum ignorantia*, ed. M. Capelli (Paris, 1906), 45, trans. and quoted in Theodore E. Mommsen, "Petrarch's Conception of the 'Dark Ages'" *Speculum* 17, no. 2 (1942): 227.

> "Dark Age," now became the time of "light" which had to be "restored"; the era following Antiquity, on the other hand, was submerged in obscurity.[15]

The movement of rebirth, or Renaissance, was then an attempt to bring about a new golden age that would recover what had been lost from centuries of neglect.

In the early sixteenth century, when Martin Luther found himself in need of a theory of history that would justify his break with the Roman Catholic Church, this model lie waiting. Luther, Philip Melanchthon, and other Reformers adopted an understanding of the Christian past (and not just the literary or artistic past) in which *decline* played a significant role. In contrast to the successionist approach in which the historian was tasked with explaining how perceived change is not, in fact, substantial change at all, the Reformers' supersessive approach to history rested upon change—especially corrosive change. They all claimed that Christian history began in a primitive purity that was corrupted through the centuries and was eventually restored and renewed in their respective reform efforts.

Perhaps the most famous and thoroughly executed example of this new approach to the Christian past was put forth by Matthias Flacius and the cadre of scholars he organized to author the massive *Magdeburg Centuries* (covering thirteen centuries in fourteen volumes, published between 1559 and 1574). In the *Centuries*, Flacius and his coauthors advanced the thesis of Christianity's decline from purity into the decadence of Catholicism (*Abfalltheorie*).[16] This approach to the Christian past was necessary to justify the Reformers' break from the historical continuity claimed by the Roman Catholic Church. It characterized many of the centuries

[15] Mommsen, "Petrarch's Conception of the 'Dark Ages,'" 228.

[16] Cf. Gregory B. Lyon, "Baudouin, Flacius, and the Plan for the Magdeburg Centuries," *Journal of the History of Ideas* 64, no. 2 (2003): 253–72.

between the New Testament and the present in terms of faithlessness that could be undone by reform efforts in the present.

Though all of the Protestant Reformers used this approach, they diverged substantially in the details. The Reformers differed in where they located the primitive purity of the church and in terms of their respective interpretations of when and how the church fell into corruption. To take one of the more extreme instances, the Swiss Reformers were inclined to locate corruption quite early. In Heinrich Bullinger's 1539 *Origin of Error*, he was bold enough to reject most of the church fathers.[17] He prioritized church fathers who were earlier, but especially ones who could be marshaled in support of the stark and simple liturgical forms of Reformed Christianity. He rejected out of hand any author who seemed to him to support more elaborate eucharistic prayers or to affirm some notion of a real presence in the eucharistic meal (e.g., the second-century authors cited previously).[18] The Anabaptist Reformers took this supersessive approach to history even further and attempted to reestablish what they understood to be the abandoned purity of the New Testament. For example, Menno Simons, the founder of the Mennonites, hoped that, with his movement, "that most holy city and temple, which lay desolated for so many centuries, may again be rebuilt, and all its usages, ordinances and services restored to primitive order."[19]

These early modern instances of the primitivism are not distinct from earlier reform movements, such as the Franciscans, in

[17] For example, Heinrich Bullinger, *De Origine Erroris* (Zurich: In Officina Froschoviana, Mense Martio, 1539), fols. 202–5, accessed September 16, 2019, https://doi.org/10.3931/e-rara-2603.

[18] Bullinger, *De Origine Erroris*, fols. 202–5; cf. Euan Cameron, "Primitivism, Patristics, and Polemic in Protestant Visions of Early Christianity," in *Sacred History: Uses of the Christian Past in the Renaissance World*, ed. Katherine Van Liere, Simon Ditchfield, and Howard Louthan (Oxford: Oxford University Press, 2012), 36.

[19] Menno Simons, "A Fundamental Doctrine," in *The Complete Works of Menno Simon, First Part* (Elkhart, IN: John F. Funk & Brother, 1871), 243.

their insistence that at the fount of Christianity there is a resource that is of paramount importance in the present. Rather, they are distinct in their supersessive judgment that there was a fall into darkness in the centuries spanning that origin to the present. Although we tend to think of most of these movements in the sixteenth century as "reforming" movements, in their supersessive approach to the Christian past, they are all to a certain extent restorationist or primitivist. Primitivism as a theological approach to Christian history, then, is not, in fact, primitive; it is not ancient. It is, in fact, "a hidden or barely recognized aspect of the modern."[20]

Primitivism rejects historical conditioning, claiming instead to bring the normative past into the present without historical mediation. The allure of this impulse is in its promise of stability and authority. In the midst of the vicissitudes of history, the primitivist finds secure footing in a normative past. It is a flight from history into an imagined stability. It is thus unsurprising that the New World, with its vast frontier, appeared to many an ideal place to escape the trappings of history and return to the primitive purity of a golden age. "The Atlantic is a Lethean stream," wrote Henry David Thoreau, "in our passage over which we have had an opportunity to forget the Old World and its institutions."[21] More than two centuries before Thoreau's comments, John Winthrop observed the same opportunity for new beginnings that the New World presented, encouraging the Puritan migrants aboard the *Arbella* that "we shall be as a city upon a hill," shining for all the world to see.[22] America was a land without a history, or rather,

[20] E. Brooks Holifield and Sidney E. Mead, "Puritan and Enlightenment Primitivism: A Response," in *The American Quest for the Primitive Church*, 73.

[21] Henry David Thoreau, "Walking," *The Atlantic*, June 1862, accessed November 9, 2019, https://www.theatlantic.com/magazine/archive/1862/06/walking/304674/.

[22] John Winthrop, "A Modell of Christian Charity (1630)," in *Collections of the Massachusetts Historical Society*, 3rd series, vol. 7 (Boston: Little & Brown, 1838), 47.

it was perceived by its European colonizers as a land without a history. This unique space afforded Puritans the opportunity to escape the corruptions that had beset the Christian faith and to restore the true, original faith.

These twin themes of escaping corruption and restoring purity were major themes in the histories that the Puritans wrote about themselves. Edward Johnson opened his optimistic (even polemical) account of the Puritan history from 1628 until 1652 by writing:

> Let the matter and form of your Churches be such as were in the Primitive Times (before Antichrist's Kingdom prevailed) plainly pointed out by Christ and his Apostles, in most of their Epistles, to be neither National nor Provincial, but gathered together in Covenant of such a number as might ordinarily meet together in one place, and built of such living stones as outwardly appear Saints by calling.[23]

Here are all the elements of a primitivist approach to the Christian past: a primal purity followed by an extended period of decay, when "Antichrist's Kingdom prevailed," which can now be corrected in the present.

Ideas of America as the site of the restoration of the true church, true humanity, or true nature pervade the writings of early European Americans, from the Puritans to the founding fathers of the republic. They saw America as a blank slate—a place where the corruption of European culture and religion could be cast aside. In the famous words of John Locke, "in the beginning, all the world

[23] Edward Johnson, *Wonder-Working Providence of Sions Saviour in New England* (London, 1654), ed. J. Franklin Jameson, Original Narratives of Early American History (New York: Scribner, 1910), 25–26. I have updated the spelling of some of the words in this quotation to reflect contemporary spelling conventions. I have retained the original capitalization.

was America."[24] From their first appearance on the American continent, Protestant Christians appropriated images of restoration and primitive purity. The great scholar of American religious history David Edwin Harrell rightly observed that the primitivist (or restorationist) sentiment "may be the most vital single assumption underlying the development of American Protestantism."[25] Indeed, Methodists, Moravians, Puritans, Episcopalians, Baptists, Charismatics, new religious movements, and others all claimed to have cast aside the shackles of centuries of ecclesial corruption and returned Christianity to its pure form.

A Critique of Primitivism

Primitivist interpretations of Christian history are an invention of the modern world. Despite some positive aspects of these interpretations that correct the successionism that prevailed for centuries, they remain historically incoherent and theologically catastrophic. Thus they should be replaced with more nuanced, mature interpretations of Christian history.

What exactly do I mean when I say that primitivism is historically incoherent? The most immediate problem that primitivism faces is the sheer number of people and movements who claim to have restored the true, pure church from its fall into corruption. Each of these groups has different interpretations of what the pure, primitive Christianity was, so they naturally differ on how they believe that purity should be expressed today. Charismatic movements have argued that the supernatural spiritual gifts and open, egalitarian structure of the church in its first decades was stymied by the development of a rigid liturgy and polity. For these movements, the pure, primitive Christianity that should

---

[24] John Locke, *Second Treatise of Government*, ch. 5, §49, ed. C. B. Macpherson (Indianapolis: Hackett, 1980), 29.

[25] David Edwin Harrell, "Epilogue," in *The American Quest for the Primitive Church*, 239.

be restored is a vibrant spiritualist movement open to theological improvisation. Baptists held that the simple essence of the biblical message of individual salvation by faith had been lost and could be restored through expository preaching. The Oxford Movement of the 1830s in England contended that the original purity of Christianity persisted in the Anglican church against the innovations of Protestantism on the one hand and corruptions of Roman Catholicism on the other, existing as a kind of historically grounded middle way (via media). And, of course, the founders of the Stone-Campbell Movement sought to restore the unity of the New Testament church through an approach to Scripture that sought its plain meaning, avoiding later doctrines and creeds as merely human creations that contribute to Christian division. One could add countless more denominations and movements to this list. The staggering variety of primitive Christianities that have been appealed to should render any claim to have recovered *the* pure form of early Christianity suspect.

All of these attempts to repristinate the church by abandoning culture and presuppositions are based upon self-deception. They attempt to escape the historical conditions of human creatureliness. Primitivism can only proceed based on the belief—well intentioned, to be sure—that humans can, in the words of Henry Warner Bowden, "by taking thought, add a cubit to their stature or, by making an effort, determine their nature and destiny."[26]

The invariable result of these attempts is that the pristine, primitive church is remade into the image of its seeker. Thomas and Alexander Campbell opened the Scriptures in search of the New Testament church. What they found in its pages was a remarkably Protestant and American voluntary association of rationalists not unlike themselves. They read the New Testament, especially Acts and the epistles, as if they were analogous to the constitution of

[26] Henry Warner Bowden, "Perplexity over a Protean Principle: A Response," in *The American Quest for the Primitive Church*, 177–78.

their new republic. They sought to read the Bible as though no one had read it before, but in casting aside the accumulated wisdom of eighteen centuries of Christian interpretation, they left themselves vulnerable to an eisegesis of self-deception. Throughout the history of the Stone-Campbell Movement, the New Testament has often been spoken of as the source of the highest authority in the church. But in practice, the New Testament has often been treated merely as a way to confirm positions already settled in the minds of its readers. The divisive history of the movement leaves no other interpretation plausible.

George Tyrell's excoriating description of the historical work of German liberal Protestant historians such as Adolf von Harnack is fitting here. Tyrell wrote that Harnack believed:

> The Pearl of Great Price fell into the dustheap of Catholicism, not without the wise permission of Providence, desirous to preserve it till the day when Germany should rediscover it and separate it from its useful but deplorable accretions. Thus between Christ and early Catholicism there is not a bridge but a chasm. Christianity did not cross a bridge; it fell into the chasm and remained there, stunned, for nineteen centuries.[27]

In Tyrell's estimation, Harnack and liberal Protestantism's presupposition that primitive Christianity fell into corruption blinded them from seeing anything but pale reflections of themselves when they opened the New Testament. "With eyes thus preoccupied," Tyrell continues, "they could only find the German in the Jew; a moralist in a visionary, a professor in a prophet; the nineteenth century in the first."[28] Tyrell concludes that "the Christ that Harnack sees, looking back through nineteen centuries of

[27] George Tyrell, *Christianity at the Crossroads* (London: Longmans, Green, & Company, 1913), 40–41.

[28] Tyrell, *Christianity at the Crossroads*, 42.

Catholic darkness, is only the reflection of a Liberal Protestant face, seen at the bottom of a deep well."[29] Such a criticism leveled at liberal academic historians like Harnack could just as easily be applied to numerous forms of conservative and fundamentalist Protestants and revisionist Catholics, each of whom fall prey to the temptation to see in the earliest form of Christianity a justification of their own theological and ecclesiastical positions.

Beyond the inevitability of remaking the past into their own image, the primitivist's narrative of supersessionism requires the swallowing of a difficult theological claim. Can it be said that God allowed the world to be absent a faithful witness for centuries? Was Christ speaking the truth when he promised to be with the disciples "always, to the end of the age" (Matt. 28:20)? The New Testament speaks of the "deposit" of faith. Was that deposit truly absent from the world for generations, hiding in the words scribbled on the yellowed pages of biblical manuscripts waiting for someone intrepid enough to read them? To be sure, some primitivist Christians have stared unflinchingly at the truth that their approach to history requires them to accept that dozens of centuries of human history passed in which the salvation that God offers through Jesus Christ was absent from humanity, lying dormant until these primitivists' present.

Others have found this to be a theological pill too difficult to swallow and so have created theories in which their understanding of the true form of Christianity was mediated through history via a series of minority groups and sects—"faithful remnants"—that were maligned and persecuted by the mainstream Catholic Church. Baptists James Robinson Graves and James Madison Pendleton advanced the theory of Landmarkism in the middle of the nineteenth century.[30] An aspect of this theory, articulated in

---

[29] Tyrell, *Christianity at the Crossroads*, 44.

[30] Cf. Hugh Wamble, "Landmarkism: Doctrinaire Ecclesiology among Baptists," *Church History* 33, no. 4 (1964): 429–77.

Pendleton's 1856 essay *An Old Landmark Reset*, was that Baptist churches were the only extant New Testament churches, the end of a long succession of persecuted faithful who were Baptist in all but name.[31]

Pendleton's genealogy for Baptists included Montanists, Novatians, Donatists, Albigensians, and Waldensians. Indeed, it was a veritable role call for heretical and schismatic groups throughout Christian history. These diverse groups hold little in common with one another in doctrine or practice. They simply share in the status that they had been rejected and condemned. This argument was an attempt to revive an aspect of the successive approach to history—continuity—through an appeal to an ever-present faithful remnant. It is an understandable response to the theological problems posed by a supersessive approach to the past, but it is without historical warrant. It is an attempt to claim a historical basis for an ahistorical theology and practice.

To be fair to Pendleton and the Landmark Baptist movement, they were not the first to articulate such an untenable historical genealogy. Nearly two decades before he published *Old Landmark Reset*, a famous Protestant minister stood before a capacity crowd in Cincinnati and claimed that

> the disciples of Christ are the same race, call them Christians, Nazarenes, Galileans, Novatians, Donatists, Paulicians, Waldenses, Albigenses, Protestants, or what you please. A variety of designation affects not the fact which we allege; we can find an unbroken series of Protestants—a regular succession of those who protested against the corruptions of the Roman church, and endeavored to hold fast the faith once delivered to the

[31] J. M. Pendleton, *An Old Landmark Reset*, 1854, reprinted in *Pillars of Orthodoxy, or Defenders of the Faith*, ed. Ben Bogard (Louisville: Baptist Book Concern, 1900), 253–66.

> saints, from the first schism in the year 250, A. D. to the present day; and you may apply to them what description or designation you please.[32]

Alexander Campbell employed this approach to history in a debate with the Roman Catholic bishop John Purcell to undermine the Catholic claim to historical continuity. Though such an approach might make it easier to have confidence in the viability of the primitivist position, it requires an imagination a good deal more creative than the most ardent conspiracy theorist's.

Overcoming Primitivism

Given the historical and theological problems with primitivism outlined here, what are the inheritors of a primitivist tradition—note the irony of the phrase—to do? We must develop a historically responsible and theologically coherent approach to the Christian past. Those of us who are inheritors of the Stone-Campbell Movement need not abandon the vision of the founders of the movement when we recognize that the ways they appealed to the past were often deeply flawed. Keith Stanglin's essay in this volume articulates a positive reinterpretation of the vision of the Stone-Campbell Movement that would accord with what I am suggesting. Elsewhere, I have suggested that because the Stone-Campbell Movement has eschewed complex doctrinal confessions that other traditions have embraced, it is perhaps capable of fostering historical and theological work that can bring about a greater understanding between traditions and ultimately greater

---

[32] Alexander Campbell and John B. Purcell, *A Debate on the Roman Catholic Religion* (Cincinnati: Benziger, 1837), 77; cf. Herbert Dean Miller, "Enacting Theology, Americanism, and Friendship: The 1837 Debate on Roman Catholicism between Alexander Campbell and Bishop John Purcell" (PhD diss., University of Dayton, 2015), 120–24.

Christian unity.[33] We must develop a historically responsible and theologically coherent approach to the Christian past. To start, we must accept that the supersessive approach to the past employed by the advocates of primitivism is neither historically nor theologically tenable. At the same time, such an approach to the past is, to an extent, an improvement upon the simplistic narratives of successionism, insofar as it recognizes the reality of historical change.

In his important book on Catholic responses to changing historical consciousness in the modern period, Owen Chadwick described the successive approach to the Christian past. If a Roman Catholic theologian in the seventeenth or eighteenth century were to be asked what the Catholic faith is, Chadwick argued, they would say that it is the "unchanging gospel, handed down by pen and mouth from age to age, generation to generation, mother to child, teacher to taught, pulpit to pew. An inexhaustible treasure deposited in a bank, so that all may draw from it. That which has been believed in every place, in every century, by all Christian men and women. *Semper Eadem*."[34] This notion of a church that never changes, never develops, never grows, and never reforms is just as historically and theologically untenable as primitivism. History clearly demonstrates that Christianity does change; its doctrines and practices develop.[35] Of course, change should come as no surprise, given the organic images for the church in the New Testament.

Unlike the successive approach to history, primitivist approaches do not have to fear acknowledging change and

---

[33] Stephen Lawson, "Historical Theology and the Stone-Campbell Movement," *Restoration Quarterly* 60, no. 1 (2018): 41–48.

[34] Owen Chadwick, *From Bossuet to Newman*, 2nd ed. (Cambridge: Cambridge University Press, 1987), 1.

[35] For a Catholic scholar's attempt to make sense of changes and developments in the Catholic Church's teaching (e.g., on usury and slavery), see John T. Noonan Jr., *A Church That Can and Cannot Change* (Notre Dame, IN: University of Notre Dame Press, 2005).

contingency in history. They do not have to explain how perceived changes in teaching or failures in practice are not actually substantial changes. Primitivists' position requires that they accept the reality of historical change and even failure in the Christian past. This is certainly an improvement in that it allows for a truthful telling of the many changes and failures of Christians to fully embody their calling that have persisted since the days of the apostles. The problem with primitivism is the claim that such change, even sin, necessitates a fall and recovery narrative *that insulates a particular ecclesial group from historical change and sin*. In this way, primitivism is driven by the same temptation that successionism is: to protect a particular tradition from the instability of history.

The way forward must begin with a theology of history, a confidence that God is not bound to the limitations of finite human history, that contingent history has been transcended through the revelation of God in Jesus Christ, that the persistence of change in God's creation does not cancel God's sustaining and directing of the cosmos to its ultimate fulfillment in which "God will be all in all" (1 Cor. 15:28). Such a theology of history does not need to fear change and can even affirm development in doctrine and practice.

In reflecting upon the development of Trinitarian doctrine in the early church, Robert Louis Wilken observed that "the truth arrives through time."[36] It took early Christians centuries to work out the implications of what the Easter event meant for their belief in God. This is not something that they concealed, claiming that the apostles articulated a full-throated Trinitarian theology by Easter evening. In theology, as Gregory of Nazianzus wrote, "growth towards perfection comes through additions."[37] He continued:

---

[36] Wilken, *Spirit of Early Christian Thought*, 101.

[37] Gregory of Nazianzus, "Oration 31," §26, translated in Gregory of Nazianzus, *On God and Christ: The Five Theological Orations and Two Letters*

> It was dangerous for the Son to be preached openly when the Godhead of the Father was still unacknowledged. It was dangerous, too, for the Holy Spirit to be made (and here I use a rather rash expression) an extra burden, when the Son had not been received. It could mean men jeopardizing what did lie within their powers, as happens to those encumbered with a diet too strong for them or who gaze at sunlight with eyes as yet too feeble for it. No, God meant it to be by piecemeal additions, "ascents" as David called them, by progress and advance from glory to glory, that the light of the Trinity should shine upon more illustrious souls.[38]

As the church comes to reflect more deeply on the revelation of God in Jesus Christ, deeper truths are revealed in an organic process. This is why, according to Gregory, the divinity of the Holy Spirit was recognized only after the full divinity of the Father and Son were clearly affirmed. Gregory had no fear of doctrinal development or historical change. To be sure, changes or developments need to be justified, but there is a profound trust at work in Gregory's theology of history: the firm belief that God is guiding the church to the fullness of truth.

This is a stark contrast to at least one famous successionist approach to the Trinitarian debates: John Henry Newman's treatment of the Arian controversy (written when he was still an Anglican). In it, he argued for a *disciplina arcani* (secret tradition), a set of teachings originating with the apostles and passed on through verbal tradition for those mature enough to understand.

to Cledonius, trans. Frederick Williams and Lionel Wickham, Popular Patristics (Crestwood, NY: St. Vladimir's Seminary Press, 2002), 137.

[38] Gregory of Nazianzus, "Oration 31," §26.

This tradition contained the fullness of the Trinitarian theology articulated by the councils of Nicaea and Constantinople.[39]

To be sure, accepting change and development in doctrine and practice necessarily raises some difficult questions about what kinds of developments are legitimate and what areas are subject to development. Is the universal adoption of the mono-episcopate in the early church binding on all Christians everywhere? Should the church exercise any temporal power, or are such developments in Christian history, from Constantine onward, always to be understood as illegitimate developments of Christian teaching? Should the biblical and early Christian teaching on violence render suspect all attempts to appeal to development to justify Christians' participation in war and violence? To these thorny questions, we could add dozens more: the nature of Christ's presence in the Eucharist, the age and mode of baptism, the nature of ordination and marriage, the status of Jewish people, and the use of instruments and iconography in the church's worship, to name just a few.

Newman famously reversed course from the successionist position he advocated as an Anglican, coming to believe that doctrine does develop and authentically does so only in the Roman Catholic Church (to which he converted in 1845).[40] Yet coming to accept that authentic change and development exist does not mean that every contested issue will be settled. Philip Schaff, the great German American Protestant church historian of the nineteenth century, wrote a book in defense of doctrinal development around the same time that Newman did, coming to significantly different conclusions than his English contemporary.[41]

---

[39] John Henry Newman, *Arians of the Fourth Century* (1833, repr., London: Longmans, Green, & Company, 1897), 50–56.

[40] John Henry Cardinal Newman, *An Essay on the Development of Christian Doctrine*, 6th ed. (Notre Dame, IN: University of Notre Dame, 1989 [1st ed. 1845]).

[41] Philip Schaff, *What Is Church History? A Vindication of the Idea of Historical Development* (Philadelphia: Lippincott, 1846).

All these issues foreground the question of authority. If the Christian past is authoritative in some sense—and I cannot see how one can say otherwise without abandoning Scripture—then which narrative of the Christian past is authoritative and in what way? How should ecclesial authority function in the present as a mediation or interpretation of this authoritative history?[42]

To address these issues with anything approaching the treatment they deserve would require many hundreds of pages more than I have here. My intention in this essay has been more targeted: to contextualize and critique approaches to the Christian past that flee from historical contingency, either by insisting upon the unchangeability of Christian truth in time or by invoking a fall narrative. Surely the first step toward a Christian understanding of history is to disabuse Christians of historically untenable and theologically deleterious approaches to the past.

[42] For more on these questions, see Jeffrey Cary, *Free Churches and the Body of Christ: Authority, Unity, and Truthfulness* (Eugene, OR: Cascade, 2012).

5

Reading Scripture Baptismally

Scott Adair

Churches of Christ lie between two Christian worlds concerning baptism.[1] With Roman Catholics, Eastern Orthodox, Anglicans, and some mainline Protestants, we believe that baptism is necessary for salvation. As the Nicene Creed (381) puts it, we too acknowledge "one baptism for the remission of sins."[2] On the other hand, with many evangelicals, we insist that baptism is only for believers. We have a high view of baptism, similar to the former, and a high view of faith, similar to the latter. But we reject the former's low view of faith at the time of baptism and the latter's low view of baptism at the time of faith.

Yet our baptismal theology is not the result of picking and choosing what we like from different traditions. It comes from

[1] This essay is adapted and substantially augmented from Scott Adair, "Reading Scripture Baptismally," *Christian Studies* 31 (2019): 17–28.

[2] John H. Leith, *Creeds of the Churches*, 3rd ed. (Louisville: John Knox Press, 1982), 33.

our approach to Scripture, our patternistic restoration hermeneutic.[3] "Doing and saying what the New Testament church did and said" has fine-tuned our convictions about baptism, but this way of reading Scripture has its blind spots. Based on the polarity and divisiveness in our movement, apparently our hermeneutic has not been effective in helping us navigate controversies.

Our patternism has not always enabled us to clearly distinguish between essential doctrines and matters of expedience. But Scripture itself elevates certain teachings as more important than others. Some of these distillations of essential truths in Scripture are doctrinal in nature, like the "seven ones" (Eph. 4:4–7) and what Paul received and passed on "as of first importance" (1 Cor. 15:3).[4] Some are ethical, like the golden rule (Matt. 7:12) and the commandment of love (Rom. 13:9–10). Some are both, like the Shema (Deut. 6:4; Mark 12:29).

A problematic patternism shows up in two ways: (1) demanding adherence to peripheral teachings as if they were central or (2) allowing too much leeway when it comes to core teachings. Until we address these problems in our approach to Scripture, we will continue to isolate ourselves and split churches. What the Churches of Christ need is an agreed-upon theological center, a lens through which to read Scripture. We need an authoritative summary that lays out for us the apostles' core teachings.

The answer may be nearer than we think. There is an overlooked summary of the Christian faith inherent in baptism. While we have a thoroughgoing theology *about* baptism, we have overlooked the theology *in* baptism. Restorationists should read Scripture baptismally, not just baptize scripturally. This initiating rite is not arbitrary. It is not simply a hoop to jump through or a

---

[3]Keith D. Stanglin, "The Restoration Movement, the Habit of Schism, and a Proposal for Unity," *Christian Studies* 28 (2016): 10.

[4]Throughout this essay, biblical text translations are those of the ESV.

test of obedience that is void of content. It is freighted with essential truths about the divine story one is entering.

We understand this principle when it comes to the Lord's Supper. We recognize that the bread and the wine communicate central truths about Christ. But we have not been as astute with baptism. When we limit our baptismal theology to precise instructions about moving into salvation, we fail to see that this rite is a distillation of the whole Christian system.

With just the slightest adjustment of perspective, one can see the central tenets of Christian faith compressed, stored, expressed, and enjoined upon the church in this (un)systematic theology called baptism. It is "unsystematic" because it is not linear, not systematized. Yet it is "systematic" because it stores information about each of the main categories that traditional systematic theology covers. Understood in this way, the enduring ordinance of baptism is more than just a "salvation issue." In ritual form, it makes claims about God (theology), Christ (Christology), the Holy Spirit (pneumatology), the church (ecclesiology), humanity (anthropology), hope (eschatology), and salvation (soteriology).

In the first and largest part of this chapter, I unpack the doctrinal content of baptism, noting how this material compares with other summaries recognized in the broader Christian tradition. Then, I demonstrate that each tenet has an ethical corollary. Baptism tells us not only what to believe but also how to live.

Baptism as Summary of Core Beliefs

Baptism—that is, the entire event of baptism and the words that accompany it—provides a comprehensive encapsulation of the Christian faith. It instructs the church and binds upon it the core content of the apostolic message through its invocation, confessions, and symbolic actions. And this content is consistent with that found in later summaries, such as the rule of faith and the Apostles' Creed.

Invoking the Triune Name

First, baptism done in the name of the Father, the Son, and the Holy Spirit initiates one into a faith that is distinctly and unapologetically Trinitarian. This trifold invocation of God's name lays out the basic outline of the Christian system. Whether sprinkling, pouring, or immersing, invoking the name of the Father, the Son, and the Holy Spirit has been a ubiquitous feature of the practice throughout Christian history and across denominational lines.

Some might point out that the very earliest baptisms did not adhere to this triune formula. For example, Acts reports that converts were baptized "in the name of Jesus Christ" (e.g., 2:38, 10:48). But this fact is not at odds with the triune invocation. It is consistent with it. The inner logic of the name "Jesus Christ" retains the Trinitarian contours of the apostolic message. The honorific "Christ," or "Anointed One," points to the "beginning of the gospel" (Mark 1:1), when the Father anointed the Son with the Holy Spirit in the Jordan (Mark 1:9–11). This scene, this opening act at the Jordan River, links baptism with the Trinity.[5]

This triune invocation most naturally explains the origin of the three-limbed formulation of the Roman Symbol, a baptismal confession in the West that found its final form in the Apostles' Creed.[6] When comparing the baptism described in the *Didache*

---

[5] Kilian McDonnell demonstrates that the baptism of Jesus was the dominant baptismal metaphor for the first three centuries of the church, as witnessed in patristic reflection as well as early Christian art. *The Baptism of Jesus in the Jordan: The Trinitarian and Cosmic Order of Salvation* (Collegeville, MN: Liturgical, 1996).

[6] The provenance of the Apostles' Creed or, even more so, the rule of faith is not as simple as I have stated here. Determining exactly how the origins of the proclamation, early creeds, hymns, liturgical confessions, baptismal formula, Roman Symbol, pre-baptismal catechism, rule of faith, councils, and Apostles' Creed relate to each other is likely not possible. Nevertheless, this has not stopped some from trying. See Tomas Bokedal, "The Rule of Faith: Tracing Its Origins," *Journal of Theological Interpretation* 7 (2013): 233–55; Everett Ferguson, *The Rule of Faith: A Guide* (Eugene, OR: Cascade, 2015), 48–65.

(80–120) to the practice in the *Apostolic Tradition* (200–215), one can see the movement from triune invocation to a three-part interrogatory creed, which is almost identical in content to the declaratory Apostles' Creed. Echoing the great commission, the *Didache* instructs, "Concerning baptism, baptize in this way. Having first rehearsed all these things, baptize in the name of the Father, and of the Son, and of the Holy Ghost, in living water."[7] The following excerpt from the *Apostolic Tradition* shows how the succinct invocation expanded to form the outline of the baptismal creed:

> When each of them to be baptized has gone down into the water, the one baptizing shall lay hands on each of them, asking, "Do you believe in God, the Father Almighty?" And the one being baptized shall answer, "I believe." He shall then baptize each of them once, laying his hand upon each of their heads.
>
> Then he shall ask, "Do you believe in Jesus Christ, the Son of God, who was born of the Holy Spirit and the virgin Mary, who was crucified under Pontius Pilate, died, and rose on the third day living from the dead, and ascended into heaven, and sat down at the right hand of the Father, the one coming to judge the quick and the dead?" When each has answered, "I believe," he shall baptize a second time.
>
> Then he shall ask, "Do you believe in the Holy Spirit, and the holy church, and the resurrection of the flesh?" Then each being baptized shall answer, "I believe." And thus let him baptize the third time.[8]

---

[7] *Didache* 7, in *Documents of the Christian Church*, ed. Henry Bettenson and Chris Maunder, 4th ed. (London: Oxford University Press, 2011), 68.

[8] Gregory Dix and Henry Chadwick, *The Treatise on the Apostolic Tradition of St. Hippolytus of Rome, Bishop and Martyr* (London: Alban, 1992), 36.

The trifold invocation is also consistent with the church fathers' heresy-fighting efforts. When distortions of the apostolic message threatened the young church from within, bishops and theologians based their polemic on the three-pronged rule of faith, the sum of the Christian gospel.[9] Thus the standard by which new teachings were measured was always Trinitarian.

As such, baptism in the name of the Father, Son, and Holy Spirit is a primary basis for Christian unity, not simply because of the shared words and forms but also because these point to the nonnegotiable Trinitarian faith that is unmistakably and unashamedly Christian. Trinitarian baptism as the foundation for unity is not foreign to the New Testament. When Paul pleads for unity in Ephesians 4:4–7, the divine persons and baptism comprise four of the seven "ones." Baptism relates directly to the remaining three "ones" of Ephesians 4:4–7, as well: "one body," "one hope," "one faith." The last section of this paper will demonstrate how these seven "ones" confirm that the teachings of the faith found in baptism are, indeed, the essential teachings.

In keeping with the historic church, Restorationists too have typically invoked "Father, Son, and Holy Spirit" at baptism, though sometimes unaware that the divine name provides the threefold outline for the core content of the gospel. Yet Restorationists, who have been so intent on baptizing scripturally, have too often failed to read Scripture baptismally. I am convinced that had Barton Stone and his heirs read Scripture through the filter of "Father, Son, and Spirit," they would have seen the interrelatedness of God

---

[9]Ferguson, *Rule of Faith*, 1–15, essentially provides a rule of faith reader with examples from the works of Irenaeus, Tertullian, Origen, and others. While it may be difficult to establish first-century baptismal invocation (e.g., Matt. 28:19) as the root of the rule of faith, it is uncontroversial to say that it is consistent with the rule of faith.

as the stage on which the drama of Scripture unfolds. As such, they would have been spared their Arian leanings.[10]

Confessing Jesus as Lord

Second, baptism encapsulates the core content of Christian faith through its confessions or creeds. Baptism and creeds were united very early in church history. Jaroslav Pelikan explains, "Because the proclamation of the kerygma and the administration of baptism belonged together, creeds were made necessary also by the demand of Christian baptism 'in the name of the Father, Son, and Holy Spirit' or 'in the name of Christ.'"[11] Even today, a Christological confession almost always accompanies the practice. This is certainly true in the Churches of Christ, which points to the fact that Restorationists, technically speaking, are not anticreedal.[12] In fact, Churches of Christ require a creed at the time of baptism: "I believe Jesus is the Son of God." This is typically expressed by affirming an interrogatory creed: "Do you believe Jesus is the Son of God?" Christological creeds, such as this one, undoubtedly go back to the very earliest Christian experience. Regarding the confession "Jesus is the Son of God" from Acts 8:37, Tomas Bokedal says, "This Western reading may . . . be our earliest extant

---

[10] For a discussion of Barton Stone's rejection of the Son's eternal existence and coequality with the Father, see Robert D. Cornwall, "Christology," in *Encyclopedia of the Stone-Campbell Movement*, ed. Paul M. Blowers, Anthony L. Dunnavant, Douglas A. Foster, D. Newell Williams (Grand Rapids: Eerdmans, 2004), 204. In the same volume, however, Newell Williams notes that Stone denied the "Arian" and "Socinian" labels that others gave him and made efforts to distinguish his views from such heresies. "Barton Warren Stone," 701, 710–12.

[11] Jaroslav Pelikan, *Credo: Historical and Theological Guide to Creeds and Confessions of Faith in the Christian Tradition* (New Haven, CT: Yale University Press, 2003), 379.

[12] The Restoration framers were only opposed to human-made creeds. See, for example, William B. Decker, "Baptismal Confession," *Restoration Quarterly* 1 (1957): 184.

baptismal profession of faith, indicating that the Christ-confession was associated with baptism from the beginning."[13]

The New Testament reflects more than just one creedal formula spoken at the time of baptism. Abraham Malherbe asserts that Romans 10:9 is a baptismal text.[14] J. N. D. Kelly points to several early single-clause Christological creeds, such as Acts 8:16, 19:5; 1 Corinthians 6:11; Romans 10:9; and Philippians 2:11.[15] There was flexibility regarding the exact wording of the confessions. While Jesus was always the primary subject, the first believers had multiple ways to verbally express their allegiance to him at baptism. The most prevalent were "Jesus is the Messiah," "Jesus is Lord," and "Jesus is the Son of God" (e.g., Mark 8:29; Acts 8:37; Rom. 10:9; 1 John 2:22). Each wording had a special emphasis, but each phrase pointed to the same reality. Given the Jewish origins of the faith, saying "Jesus is the Messiah" means saying "Jesus is the Son of God." For instance, Psalm 2:7, 2 Samuel 7:14, and Mark 1:9–11 show the connection between the Jewish understanding of the Messiah and the Son of God. In these passages, the Anointed One is also the Son of God. And confessing him to be such had costly political ramifications.

Robert Jenson captures the costly nature of Christian baptism and its attendant creeds. Jenson summarizes, "When admitting to participation in the Eucharist by baptism, God and the church needed to ask whether a candidate had grasped what he or she was taking on. And so, as the candidate took the morally revolutionary and quite possibly fatal step, the candidate would be

---

[13] Bokedal, "Rule of Faith," 242. More strongly, without Christological creeds, there is no such thing as "Christian experience."

[14] Abraham Malherbe, "New Testament Creeds and Their Uses," *Christian Studies* 14 (1994): 10.

[15] J. N. D. Kelly, *Early Christian Creeds*, 3rd ed. (New York: Longman, 1972), 14–19.

asked, 'Do you believe . . . ?'"[16] For when people confess Jesus as King, or divine Son, or Lord, they are saying that Caesar is not. The Apostles' Creed, though, rather than choosing one Christological title over another, locks in all three honorifics: "[I believe] in Jesus Christ, his only Son, our Lord."[17]

All of this is simply to say that Christian baptism, like the rule of faith and the Apostles' Creed, is Christocentric. Jesus Christ is the clear focal point of each. For example, of the twelve articles in the Apostles' Creed, six of them are about Jesus, compared to one for the Father and one for the Spirit. This is consistent with the rule of faith as well. Whether it is a version of the rule from Irenaeus, Tertullian, Origen, Clement, or anywhere else, there is always more doctrinal material dedicated to Jesus Christ than there is to any other category. The story unfolds along Trinitarian lines, but the story itself focuses on the person of Christ. So it is with Christian baptism. The spoken words of the rite are unmistakably Christocentric.

Sadly, however, Christ-centeredness has not always described how Restorationists approach Scripture as, for example, in T. W. Brents's *Gospel Plan of Salvation*.[18] This ambitious and influential volume ostensibly gave Restorationists a complete exposition of the gospel. The first 150 pages exposed the errors of Calvinist doctrines. The final 300 focused on the proper mode and function of baptism, refuting pedobaptists, non-immersionists, and anyone who does not view baptism as essential for salvation. But Doug Foster notes that the *Gospel Plan of Salvation*, in spite of its title, has nothing in it that can properly be labeled Christological.[19]

---

[16] Robert W. Jenson, *Canon and Creed*, Interpretation (Louisville: Westminster John Knox Press, 2010), 16.

[17] Leith, *Creeds of the Churches*, 24.

[18] T. W. Brents, *The Gospel Plan of Salvation* (Nashville: Gospel Advocate, 1874).

[19] Douglas A. Foster, "Christology in the Stone-Campbell Movement: An Exploratory Survey" (paper presented at the Restoration Theological

In review, when Churches of Christ baptize in the name of the Father, Son, and Spirit, confessing Jesus Christ as the Son of God or Lord, they verbalize the foundation of Christian faith, which enjoys overlap with the essential content of the rule of faith and the Apostles' Creed. All three of these historic summaries present a doctrinal core that is Trinitarian and Christocentric.

The Depths of the Symbol

Third, the symbolic act of immersion in water enjoins upon the convert and proclaims to the church, even if indirectly, the remaining basic tenets of Christian faith. Beyond theology and Christology, the ritual, as described in the New Testament, expresses other core teachings concerning the Spirit, humanity, sin, salvation, the church, and our future hope. I will continue to compare the content of baptism with the standardized language of the Apostles' Creed. The rule of faith, though, has too many variations on these matters for an essay of this length to make any meaningful further comparisons.

While some baptizers are careful to mention the promise from Acts 2:38 concerning the gift of the Holy Spirit, the sending and sealing of the Spirit is expressed in the ritual, whether verbalized or not. After all, Christian baptism finds its primary antecedent in Jesus's baptism in the Jordan (e.g., Gal. 3:26–4:7).[20] As such, Christian baptism recalls and reenacts the Trinitarian drama where the Father anoints his Son with his Spirit (Matt. 3:16–17; Mark 4:9–11; Luke 3:21–22). Just as the Father sent his Spirit to confirm Jesus's divine Sonship, so also the Father sends us his Spirit as we unite with his Son, confirming our adoption as his children. This pneumatologically rich symbol invites the church to develop from Scripture a robust doctrine of the Holy Spirit. Not unlike

Fellowship, Boston, November 20, 1999), 10.

[20] J. A. T. Robinson, "The One Baptism as a Category of New Testament Soteriology," *Scottish Journal of Theology* 6 (1953): 257–74.

baptism, the connection between water and the Spirit of God is a theme in the biblical story from beginning to end (Gen. 1:2; Rev. 22:17; see also, e.g., John 3:5; 1 John 5:7–8). To read Scripture baptismally is to recognize that this water-Spirit motif offers insights about the work of the Holy Spirit within the created order, not simply an apologetic for the necessity of baptism.

Admittedly, whether in word or symbol, the explicit pneumatological content in baptism is brief. But that is how rituals function. They compress inexhaustible concepts into a memorable symbolic action that invites further exploration. The Apostles' Creed is similarly concise: "I believe in the Holy Spirit." Jenson notes:

> One cannot, for example, forever keep saying, "Jesus died to save us from our sin," without pondering how that might work. . . . Thus sophisticated theological reflection à la Paul or the evangelist John belongs to the mission itself. One cannot keep confessing, for example, "he is Lord," without helpfully identifying the subject. Thus to remain gospel, the gospel narrative requires narrative expansion, à la the Gospels.[21]

In the same way, the creed or summary of faith needs to be fleshed out with Scripture.

In a passage of Scripture almost as familiar to Restorationists as Acts 2:38, Romans 6 connects immersion in water with the death, burial, and resurrection of Jesus. As such, being lowered and lifted from the water recalls the pivotal event of human history, the crux of the apostolic message (1 Cor. 15:3–7). The rite looks both back and forward, claiming Jesus's triumph over death is the destiny for believers and the bellwether for the cosmos (Rom. 8:18–23). The ritual is dramatized eschatology. The Apostles'

[21] Jenson, *Canon and Creed*, 41.

Creed likewise includes eschatological articles of faith: "[I believe] in the resurrection of the body, and life everlasting."

The New Testament also connects baptism with washing. In the simplest terms, baptism is a bath (1 Pet. 3:21). This washing symbolism and the phrase "for the forgiveness of sins" that Restorationists home in on say something about the nature of sin, human culpability, and the need for reconciliation (Acts 2:38, 22:16). Baptism and the gospel summarized by it engage the categories of hamartiology, anthropology, and soteriology. The Apostles' Creed follows suit: "[I believe in] the forgiveness of sin." While it might be easy to take such a pithy phrase for granted, any statement claiming to summarize Christian faith that gives no accounting for human sinfulness and its remedy is simply not Christian.

Also, it should be noted that baptism is passive. Restorationists have traditionally understood baptism as one of "the five steps" in "the plan of salvation." This five-step approach among Restorationists is traced back to Walter Scott (1796–1861), who used his five-finger exercise as a memory aid.[22] Scott pointed to each finger, starting with the thumb, and repeated the words, "faith," "repentance," "baptism," "remission of sins," and "the gift of the Holy Spirit," sometimes pairing "eternal life" with the Holy Spirit on the little finger. It also served as a contrasting response to the *ordo salutis* of Reformed soteriology.

Soon after Scott, however, a revised five-step plan emerged: hear, believe, repent, confess, and be baptized. But given the passive nature of the command to "be baptized," perhaps "step" is not the most fitting metaphor. The convert is not so much the doer or the actor as the one consenting to be acted upon. This is not just a matter of semantics. It is germane to the content of the Christian message that *one never baptizes oneself.* Someone else already

[22] See Peter Morgan, "Five Finger Exercise," in *Encyclopedia of the Stone-Campbell Movement*, 338–39.

belonging to the church bathes the convert. A private baptism or a baptism without any witnesses is thus not actually possible. At least one other person must be present, or it is not Christian baptism. This universal feature of baptism enacts the role that the church plays in mediating divine grace. One cannot bypass the church to receive Christ's benefits. The New Testament's baptismal ecclesiology is explicit and presented as a symbol of catholicity: "We were all baptized by one Spirit into one body—whether Jews or Greeks, slave or free" (1 Cor. 12:13). The Apostles' Creed also makes ecclesiological confessions: "[I believe in] the holy catholic church, the communion of saints."

Thus, in both word and symbol, baptism makes claims about theology, Christology, pneumatology, anthropology, soteriology, ecclesiology, and eschatology. It stores, expresses, and enjoins upon the church the core beliefs of the apostolic message. In the last chapter of *The Rule of Faith: A Guide*, Everett Ferguson discusses the "Relevance for Today of the Rule of Faith."[23] Since baptism and the rule of faith both summarize the same apostolic faith, it is no coincidence that every benefit to churches that Ferguson ascribes to the ancient rule of faith is also applicable to the baptismal rule I am proposing. Following Ferguson's subtitles, the rule of faith is relevant for churches today because it

- offers a succinct statement of core Christian doctrine for inquirers, new converts, and the congregation and its leaders;
- helps the church discern the center of Christian doctrine from the periphery;
- enables the church to test teachings;
- keeps the focus on the story of Christ;
- guides biblical interpretation;

[23] Ferguson, *Rule of Faith*, 83–90.

- grounds faith in history; and
- reminds the church of the coming judgment and resurrection.[24]

Nevertheless, it is not overreaching to say that leaders in the Churches of Christ, if given the two options, would typically be more favorably disposed to turn to baptism for these benefits than to the rule of faith.

Ethical Implications of the Baptismal Rule

Furthermore, beyond just doctrinal content, baptism also offers ethical content. So, once the doctrinal content of baptism is discerned, it is equally important to recognize that each tenet points to an ethical demand. Christian faith is not reducible to a list of beliefs. To become a Christian is to be initiated into a process of becoming like God. For we are "created after the likeness of God in true righteousness and holiness" and called to "be imitators of God" (Eph. 4:24, 5:1).

To that end, the essential claims of the faith should not simply communicate who God is and what he has done, but they also should tell reconciled humans how to live. Each doctrinal tenet within baptism thus has an ethical counterpart. Following the order of events for typical Restorationist baptisms, this section points out the rich ethical content laden in baptism.

The Rule of Christ

In Restorationist baptismal practice, the first thing the convert does is confess that Jesus Christ, the Son of God, is Lord. This confession acknowledges that Christ is the ruler. It is an oath of submission and allegiance to Jesus from which all Christian ethics flow. James McClendon expresses the connection in this way: "The claim that life is to be lived in *this* way—in the Christian

[24] Ferguson, *Rule of Faith*, 83–90.

way—depends on Christ's rightful lordship, his right to the mastery of our lives."[25] It is central to the Christian faith that one submits to Christ in all things, including matters of conduct and disposition. To read Scripture baptismally, then, is to read it asking the question, "How does Jesus, the ruler, want his followers to think, act, and treat others?" Matthew 5–7, for example, provides a compendium of Christ's ethical demands.

Trinitarian Love

Second, it is fitting that Christians baptize in the name of the Father, Son, and Holy Spirit since the doctrine of the Trinity is at the core of Christian faith. It is central because it reveals who God is and what he is like. It teaches that God, in his very essence, is love (1 John 5:8). He is mutually self-outpouring love.[26] God is a diversity of persons who are fully united. And this God who is love wants his covenant people to be like him. Jesus prays that believers may be one, even as he and the Father are one, so that the world may know that the Father has sent the Son (John 17:21). Chief among all ethical expectations in Scripture is that of love because it mirrors the essence of God (Mark 12:29–31; 1 John 5:11).

Dying with Christ

After taking the convert's confession and invoking the triune name, the baptizer lowers the confessor into the water. This burial in the water expresses that the convert is no longer living for himself or herself. Dying with Christ is not limited to a past event.[27] It is the ongoing feature of Christian existence. Thus baptism is an invitation to cruciform life because God is cruciform. According

---

[25] James Wm. McClendon Jr., *Ethics: Systematic Theology*, 2nd ed. (Nashville: Abingdon, 2002), 1:270; italics original.

[26] Catherine Mowry LaCugna, *God for Us: The Trinity and Christian Life* (San Francisco: HarperSanFrancisco, 1991), 382.

[27] See Robert C. Tannehill, *Dying and Rising with Christ: A Study in Pauline Theology* (Berlin: Töpelmann, 1967), 127.

to Michael J. Gorman, "the cross of Christ is not only *initiated* by God; it *reveals* God. Christ crucified is the power and wisdom of God (1 Cor. 1:18–25)."[28] The old self is crucified with Christ, and the new self rises with him to live a new life (Rom. 6:3–11; Gal. 2:20). As Christ submitted to God by immersing himself in the abyss of human fallenness, even participating in human mortality, so baptism enjoins upon the believer the mandate of obedient self-outpouring (Phil. 2:6–11). Just as Christ conquered sin and death, those who rise from the water with him are free from the control of sin and the fear of death to live virtuous, godly lives.

While Paul points back to immersion as a symbol of dying to self and rising to live a new life, there are other actions connected to the ritual that communicate the same point. Specifically, there are baptismal allusions in passages that speak of "putting off" vices like immorality, impurity, and greed, and "putting on" virtues like compassion, humility, and patience (Eph. 4:22, 24; Col. 3:5, 12). This "putting off" and "putting on" language draws upon the tangible action of removing old clothes before baptism and putting on new clothes after baptism, when the convert is clothed with Christ.

Members of Christ's Body

The convert does not enter the water alone to baptize himself or herself. He or she enters the water and is baptized with the help of another. Symbolically then, the believer not only joins Christ but also joins the church. It is typical of baptisms in Churches of Christ for someone to speak about the significance of the church in the life of the new believer, even if informally. For example, one might say, "Please remain afterward so that we can welcome our new sister (or brother) in Christ."

In fact, to join Christ *is* to join the church. Paul observes, "For just as the body is one and has many members, and all the

[28] Michael J. Gorman, *Apostle of the Crucified Lord: A Theological Introduction to Paul and His Letters* (Grand Rapids: Eerdmans, 2004), 119; italics original.

members of the body, though many, are one body, so it is with Christ. For in one Spirit we were all baptized into one body—Jews or Greeks, slaves or free—and all were made to drink of one Spirit" (1 Cor. 12:12–13). Such an invitation into divine community and the life of the church reverses the autonomous direction instigated by the fall.[29] This reality demands that all members make every effort to maintain the unity of the Spirit through the bond of peace, being humble, bearing with one another in love, and using their gifts to enrich the community (Eph. 4:3, 9–12).

Forgive as Forgiven

In Churches of Christ, nothing has been more emphasized regarding baptism than its connection with the forgiveness of sins. We often fail, however, to emphasize its ethical corollary. In a baptismal text that contains "putting off" and "putting on" language, Paul exhorts, "Be kind to one another, tenderhearted, forgiving one another, as God in Christ forgave you" (Eph. 4:32). To say, as in the Apostles' Creed, "I believe in the forgiveness of sin" is not enough. Linking forgiveness to baptism, as Churches of Christ do, is not enough. Being immersed into God's forgiveness commits one to becoming a forgiving person. As L. Gregory Jones says, "Baptism stresses the priority of forgiven-ness to our own forgiving-ness."[30] Christians are not merely recipients of God's grace; they are conduits of it.

Spirit-Empowered Ethics

Baptism is linked with the gift of the Holy Spirit. But belief in the Holy Spirit is more than a doctrine to confess. It is the habitation of a divine person who bears the fruit of godly character in

---

[29] John D. Zizioulas, *Being as Communion* (Crestwood, NY: St. Vladimir's Seminary Press, 1985), 102.

[30] L. Gregory Jones, *Embodying Forgiveness: A Theological Analysis* (Grand Rapids: Eerdmans, 1995), 174.

believers' lives (Gal. 5:22–23), enabling them to keep the ethical demands placed on them. The Holy Spirit, according to Jenson, "*is* the new life that baptism grants."[31] In so doing, God displays to the world through the church his unity, his goodness, his righteousness, and his self-outpouring love.

Character Shaped by Hope

Finally, lifting the believer out of the water points back to Christ's resurrection and forward to the ultimate resurrection and renewal in which all believers and all creation will share (Rom. 6:5, 8:19–21). But this is more than simply a truth to which one gives intellectual assent. McClendon is right when he insists that "the resurrection is central not only for doctrine but for Christian morality as well. The resurrection is the event on which all Christian existence hangs; it is the *sine qua non* of the Christian life."[32] Coming full circle to the baptismal confession of Jesus's lordship, this claim loses its meaning if Jesus was not raised from the dead. This divine act establishes the claim of Jesus's rule (Acts 5:31, 10:40–42, 13:33, 17:31). Furthermore, the promise to someday join Jesus in his resurrection sets a vision for believers so that they can begin to live out their identity as heirs of God, co-heirs with Christ. It gives shape to the ethical life of the church. J. Paul Sampley puts it this way:

> Without its eschatology—that is, without its second horizon—Paul's gospel loses its power. Fundamental to Paul's proclamation is the claim that God's re-creation, the transformation of sin-riddled creation, is underway. Paul's invitation to faith is a bid to become partakers in and heirs to what God is doing. To eradicate Paul's

---

[31] Robert W. Jenson, *Visible Words* (Philadelphia: Fortress, 1978), 157–58; italics original.

[32] McClendon, *Ethics*, 1:270; italics original.

> eschatological claims relegates his letters to the status of source books for some general counsels and bits of moralism. When one loses sight of Paul's eschatological critique of this age and its values, then the values of one's own age creep back into one's thought world and become formative.[33]

In a passage of Scripture that echoes baptism, Paul strengthens Christians' moral vision by reminding them of their resurrection with Christ:

> If then you have been raised with Christ, seek things that are above, where Christ is, seated at the right hand of God. Set your minds on things that are above, not on things that are on earth. For you have died, and your life is hidden with Christ in God. When Christ who is your life appears, then you also will appear with him in glory. Put to death, therefore, what is earthly in you: sexual immorality, impurity, passion, evil desire, and covetousness, which is idolatry. (Col. 3:1–5)

In review, Christian baptism expresses who God is, what he has done, and how redeemed humanity must live. There is no bifurcation of doctrine and ethics. The gospel entails both. Thus to read Scripture baptismally is to submit to the reign of Christ, which means living obedient, selfless, forgiving, Spirit-transformed lives of love that participate in God's mission of re-creation through the church.

Helping Churches Read Scripture Baptismally

This proposal aims for nothing short of a congregational culture change. When a local church learns to read Scripture baptismally,

---

[33] J. Paul Sampley, *Walking between the Times: Paul's Moral Reasoning* (Minneapolis: Fortress, 1991), 108.

changes will occur in terms of direction, identity, and conflict resolution. But implementing the baptismal rule requires focused and deliberate effort. So this final section maps out a strategy designed to help a congregation ground its proclamation and practices in the essentials of Christian faith that are compressed, stored, and expressed in baptism.

Translating the Proposal

In order to educate the congregation, one must make the proposal accessible. Comparing baptismal theology with the Apostles' Creed may be appropriate for an academic paper, but it would not be compelling or even comprehensible to most leaders in Churches of Christ. The proposal must be translated into laypersons' terms.

Six Adjustments in Perspective

This translation begins with a shift in perspective—a new way of seeing. The well-known illustration *My Wife and My Mother-in-Law* is an accessible reminder of the importance of perspective.[34] In order to see the drawing correctly, we must adjust how we look at it. This section offers six perspective adjustments or ways to help Restorationists see baptism and Scripture more clearly. These adjustments are represented by six key words: *pyramid*, *gospel*, *Passover*, *Jordan*, *fingers*, and *ones*.

Pyramid represents the first adjustment in perspective. As discussed earlier, Scripture prioritizes its teachings. The image of a pyramid with three sections illustrates this principle. The bottom of the pyramid is the foundation, and this foundation is made with the blocks of essential, nonnegotiable truths of Christianity. The middle section of the pyramid contains important matters (also

[34] W. E. Hill, "My Wife and My Mother-in-Law," *Puck*, November 6, 1915, 11. https://www.loc.gov/pictures/item/2010652001/.

called disputable matters, or matters of conviction, conscience, or interpretation). The top of the pyramid is for matters of preference or style. If church leaders do not accept that some Christian truths are more important than others, there is not much point in moving on to the next principle.

Gospel represents the next adjustment. The New Testament refers back to a specific message. That is, apostolic authors often allude to some earlier body of teaching to which the recipients adhered. The letters of Paul offer the following clear examples:

1. "Now I would remind you, brothers, of the gospel I preached to you, which you received, in which you stand, and by which you are being saved, if you hold fast to the word I preached to you" (1 Cor. 15:1–2).
2. "If anyone preaches a gospel other than the one you received, let him be accursed" (Gal. 1:9).
3. "Follow the pattern of the sound words that you have heard from me . . . guard the good deposit entrusted to you" (2 Tim. 1:12–14).
4. "What you have heard from me in the presence of many witnesses entrust to faithful men who will be able to teach others also" (2 Tim. 2:2).

In other words, there is a core set of teachings that established the church and held it together before there was such a thing as the New Testament. Scripture does not point to itself as the foundation of our faith but to the gospel. So we must quarry Scripture searching for the gospel before we mine it for anything else. To do so is to read Scripture baptismally.

Passover represents the third adjustment in perspective. Participatory rituals played a significant role in Judaism. For example, Passover grounded observant Jews in the story of how God delivered their forebears from captivity, assuring them that he would do it again. Showing the connection between Passover and the Lord's Supper helps Christians see that participatory rituals store identity-shaping content. There is a cautionary parable here, though. How tragic it would be for Jews to get all of the ingredients of the Seder right but forget to tell the story of God's deliverance. In the same way, churches might perform baptisms with great biblical accuracy but fail to recognize what the event says about who God is, what he has done, and how he wants his people to live.

Jordan represents the fourth change in perspective. Exploring the doctrinal content of Jesus's baptism is an indirect way to help Christians adjust the way they think about baptism. For example, it is not difficult to see all three persons of the Trinity at Jesus's baptism. And seeing most, if not all, of the essentials represented in Jesus's baptism moves hearers right up to the edge of being able to see those essentials in their own baptism.

Fingers represents the fifth way to look at baptism and Scripture differently. This adjustment helps people remember the seven essential truths of baptism by associating them with a new "five-finger exercise." It is not meant to replace the one so many Restorationists already know. It is meant to complete it. The deficiency of the old one is that there is so little attention given to the first step: *hear*. What exactly *is* the gospel that one must hear before he or she believes, repents, confesses, and is baptized? This new five-finger exercise summarizes the broad strokes of the gospel story while demonstrating its connection with the ritual of baptism. The following describes the exercise in detail, as if instructing someone how to do it.

First, hold up your thumb as if to hitchhike or affirm something and say, "Jesus Christ, the Son of God, is Lord." In Restorationist baptismal practice, taking the adherent's confession is the first part of the ceremony. Typically, one affirms the question, "Do you believe that Jesus Christ is the Son of God?," to which the believer says, "Yes." Hence the affirming thumbs-up sign is a memory aid.

Next, point your index finger to the sky (as if to indicate "number one") and say, "God, who is one, is Father, Son, and Holy Spirit," pointing to each knuckle on your index finger as you say, "Father, Son, and Holy Spirit." This corresponds with the next part of the ceremony when the baptizer invokes the name of God, baptizing in the name of the Father, Son, and Holy Spirit.

After that, express the next essential by making the peace sign, holding both the index and middle finger up in the shape of a V. With your other index finger, trace the V while saying, "I believe in the death [tracing the downward descent of the V], the burial [pausing at the bottom of the V], and the resurrection of Jesus [tracing the upward ascent of the V]."

Next, point to the fourth finger, or what some call the ring finger. This symbolizes the relational dimension of the Christian faith. The believer is committing not just to God but also to the people of God, the church, the body and bride of Christ. This is expressed in baptism by the fact that someone else, a church member, performs the baptism. Furthermore, the convert is not simply entering a local congregation but is also joining the universal church of the Lord Jesus Christ. Unlike circumcision, which excluded women and Gentiles, washing in water is an inclusive, universal practice. Baptism, then, is an expression of the unity of the church.

Then point to the pinky—the weak, short finger. This reminds us that humans are weak, that we have sinned and fallen short of the glory of God and need forgiveness. The forgiveness that the believer experiences in Christ is symbolized by being bathed in the water.

There are two essentials left, which are represented by the whole hand rather than by individual fingers. After assigning meaning to each finger, open up the same hand with the palm pointed upward, as if to receive something from heaven. This sixth gesture symbolizes that the believer receives the gift of the Holy Spirit. The connection between the Holy Spirit and baptism is seen most vividly through imagery of Jesus's baptism, which foreshadows the association of the Spirit with Christian baptism (Acts 2:38).

Finally, take that open hand and lift it straight up, like a person who is signaling for a crowd to rise. This seventh gesture reminds us of the promise of resurrection. As Jesus overcame death, those who are in him also will be raised from the dead. This hope is enacted in advance when one is lifted up from the chaotic waters of baptismal death to live a new life.

In actual practice, this new five-finger exercise has been the most important key to making this proposal accessible and memorable. When an audience works through this exercise, even just once, they start recognizing the essential truths in baptism. And they remember them.

Ones represents the seventh perspective shift. This final adjustment validates the claim that the tenets in baptism are the core tenets of Christian faith by comparing them with the "seven ones" found in Ephesians 4:4–7. Five of the seven are obvious matches. "One Lord" correlates with the confession that "Jesus Christ, the Son of God, is Lord." "One God and Father of all" correlates with the invocation of the name of God, who is "Father, Son, and Holy Spirit." "One body" corresponds to the truth that "we were all baptized into one body" (1 Cor. 12:12). "One Spirit" correlates with the "gift of the Holy Spirit." "One hope" corresponds to the promise of resurrection that is symbolized by being raised from the waters of baptism.

The last two also correlate as well but require a little explanation. "One faith" correlates with "the death, burial, and resurrection of Jesus." Surely Paul would not omit from the list of what unites all Christians the truth that he deems of first importance: "that

Christ died for our sins in accordance with the Scriptures, that he was buried, and that he was raised on the third day in accordance with the Scriptures" (1 Cor. 15:3–4). Since this is the historical crux and center of Christian faith, it might simply be called "the faith." In other words, the heart of Paul's preaching was Jesus's death and resurrection—the "one faith" that unites us.

Lastly, "one baptism" correlates with "the forgiveness of sins." When first-century Christians heard the word "baptism," it did not carry all the historic baggage it carries today. There were no fonts or baptisteries. There were no cathedrals or church buildings. There were no controversies about pedobaptism versus believers' baptism, debates over sprinkling versus immersion, or divisions regarding the necessity of baptism versus its status as optional. To the earliest adherents, in simplest terms, immersion in water was a cleansing bath. As such, it was the tangible reference to the reality of sins being washed away (Acts 22:16). To the original audience, "one baptism" sounded more like "one washing."

For Paul, these seven ones functioned as the basis for Christian unity. It may take some slight adjustments in perspective, as outlined previously. But Restorationists might also easily recognize that baptism has the same function.

Conclusion

The letters of the New Testament were written to baptized communities. Based on the number of baptismal allusions in them, it seems that the authors assumed the audience could not read or hear these letters, except baptismally. This may explain why New Testament documents do not typically argue *toward* but rather *from* baptism.

Since Churches of Christ have not had a guide or a lens that clearly identifies those basic tenets of the apostolic message, we have often allowed secondary or tertiary matters to be treated as essential issues that threaten the truth of the gospel, resulting in isolationism and division. We need an authoritative summary to help us distinguish nonnegotiable truths from other important, though not core, matters of faith. Leaders in Churches of Christ would likely affirm each statement in the Apostles' Creed as representative of the core content of the faith (although they might quibble with the phrase "he descended into hell," as others have). But it is unlikely that they would see the creed itself, in its fixed form, as authoritative. To use a prescription drug analogy, our leaders may have confidence in the powdery medication itself (the truths stated in the Apostles' Creed) but would be hesitant, if not dubious, about the capsule form in which it comes (the Apostles' Creed as a fixed, authoritative summary).

However, baptism is a capsule form that leaders in Churches of Christ already see as early, apostolic, and authoritative. They just need to acknowledge that it is not an empty shell. Once Restorationists recognize within their own practice of baptism the broad strokes of the Christian gospel, this comprehensive (un)systematic encapsulation could serve as an interpretive guide that would help us prioritize doctrines, clarify our Christian identity, and better navigate controversy. Of course, this is no panacea. In no way does it exempt leaders from the need to study Scripture, pray for wisdom, and rely on the Spirit. But if a doctrinal dispute arises among leaders who read Scripture baptismally, they could at least discern the level of the threat.

If the issue in question is not related to the content that is stored and expressed in Christian baptism—in its invocation, confessions, or symbolism—it is likely not a core tenet of the Christian faith. For example, does the dispute challenge the oneness of God as Father, Son, and Spirit? Does it deny Jesus's divinity or lordship? Does the teaching reject the presence and transforming power of the Holy Spirit? Does it undermine or deny the life, death, resurrection, or ascension of Jesus, the forgiveness of sin, the hope of resurrection, or the church as the body of Christ? If not, then it is likely not an essential matter, and it would be an affront to the truth of the gospel to divide the church over it. If leaders can discern with confidence that a matter is nonessential, they could guide the church through the controversy with the expedience, wisdom, and consideration described in Romans 14–15.

It is not difficult to find people within Churches of Christ who feel we have placed too much emphasis on baptism. Many are embarrassed because our focus on baptism has built a wall between Churches of Christ and the rest of Christendom. Not only have we isolated ourselves; we have splintered into factions within our own fellowship because our approach to Scripture has not brought clarity concerning how to distinguish essentials from nonessentials. What we have needed all along is an agreed-upon theological center—a Trinitarian, Christocentric encapsulation of apostolic faith. Yet the answer has been right under the surface the whole time. What we need is a unifying theology regarding baptism. In this respect, Churches of Christ have not focused nearly enough on this rite and its (un)systematic theological content.

6

Beyond *Sola Scriptura*: An Expanded View of Textual Inspiration

Lauren Smelser White

Since nearly its beginning, Protestantism has been beleaguered by its own convictions. A prime example of its self-inflicted beleaguerment resides in its foundational *sola scriptura* convictions that "Scripture alone" is necessary for discerning God's will and character, because the inspired text supposedly communicates the gospel's core content clearly to every faithful reader. The burden of adhering to these convictions is underscored by a persistent trend in Protestant history: however adamantly they declare the church to be "one" and "universal," Protestant fellowships tend to splinter along lines of disagreement when seemingly incompatible interpretations of Scripture arise.

Granted, for contemporary inheritors of the *sola scriptura* tradition who wish to pursue both ecumenism and the characteristically Protestant "high view" of Scripture, the situation is not hopeless. A number of Protestantism's most renowned theologians of the twentieth century have worked to forge sustainable hermeneutic paths forward. They have managed to propose interpretive paradigms that avoid the polarized dangers of fundamentalism and relativism, while retaining (some iteration of) core Protestant commitments to the priesthood of all believers and the primacy of Scripture. Such efforts have made real strides, perhaps most notably in their reaching a general consensus that the biblical text ought to be received, first and foremost, *theologically*—as the worshiping community's witness to divine acts within history—rather than in the terms of a nontheological discipline. Nevertheless, the correct way of identifying Scripture's essential theological content has remained unclear. It is obscured not least by a seemingly unending tug-of-war between ostensibly "conservative" versus "liberal" camps. These accuse one another of either rewriting the sacred text's meanings to satisfy the demands of secular culture or uncritically supporting oppressive traditionalism in the name of faithfulness.

I do not pretend to have uncovered the solution to Protestantism's contemporary hermeneutic quandaries. My objective in writing this essay is simply to sketch an honest view of the paths Protestant interpreters have taken so as to suggest where we might go. With that goal in mind, this essay's aims are threefold, culminating with a concluding recommendation for future hermeneutic engagements:

1. To sketch a rough outline of Protestantism's historical employment of *sola scriptura* thinking, thereby proposing an account of the movement's strengths and vulnerabilities;

2. To recommend, in light of that assessment, Protestant interpreters' more serious attention to the interrelationship between theology and spirituality;[1] and
3. To suggest how certain resources from this interrelationship might speak to a challenge intrinsic to the Protestant interpretive tradition.

I conclude by recommending a promising trajectory for hermeneutic practice that emerges from the intersections of theology and spirituality: an analogy of "maternal knowing." Such an analogy may prove useful for charting the church's interpretive task as a Spirit-led body, ever pursuing Scripture's transformative implications for every unfolding historical situation.

Protestantism's Early Engagement with *Sola Scriptura*

At the advent of the Protestant Reformation, Europe witnessed numerous shifts as a result of the emerging humanist theory finding its way into shared social consciousness. One momentous shift that occurred was the perceived site of doctrinal authority in relation to Scripture, which transferred from the church hierarchy to the common person.[2] The key hermeneutic distinction between the burgeoning humanist sensibility and the church's traditional framework resided in the fact that the latter understood biblical interpretation as fundamentally tied to the church's corporate

[1]For details concerning what I mean by "spirituality," the reader might refer to LeRon Shults's plenary address, wherein he says, "Broadly speaking, the theme of spirituality deals with the ways in which we interpret and attend to the transformation of our relation to God and our neighbors." See LeRon Shults, "Current Trends in Pneumatology" (conference paper, Nordic Systematic Theology Conference, Copenhagen, January 4–7, 2007).

[2]Cf. Werner G. Jeanrond, *Theological Hermeneutics: Development and Significance* (New York: Crossroad, 1991), 31.

understanding. By contrast, Christian humanists took individual biblical interpretation to be the critical mode of assessing which aspects of doctrine and practice corresponded to authentic Christian faith.[3] The Protestant Reformers came to adopt this position on the doctrinal basis that Scripture possesses *claritas*—that is, the illuminating power to clarify all things—afforded by the Holy Spirit.

The Reformers came to this understanding of Scripture under the bold leadership of Martin Luther. Luther believed he had discovered that God speaks in the gospel message to each individual more clearly than through any human teacher. Consequently, he deemed it unnecessary for illuminating commentary on Scripture to be handed down by the teaching office of the church. Luther anchored this assertion to the New Testament theme of the priesthood of all Christian believers, arguing that, in Scripture, Christ acts "alone as mediator, atoning sacrifice, high priest and intercessor."[4] Thus the only true priesthood is Christ's, in which all believers participate equally through their baptism.[5] In Luther's understanding, there remains a difference of *office* among Christians for the sake of church order, but there is no difference in each person's spiritual *rights*. One of those common spiritual rights, Luther maintained, is the knowledge of God's Word afforded by the Holy Spirit—the same Spirit who guided the penning of the Scriptures, so as to open the heart of the believer to the gospel.[6] Given the latter purpose, Luther maintained that the Spirit must be "the simplest

[3] Historians David A. Rausch and Carl Hermann Voss offer a helpful explanation of this in *Protestantism—Its Modern Meaning* (Philadelphia: Fortress, 1987), 18.

[4] Martin Luther, *Augsburg Confession*, art. 21, in *The Book of Concord: The Confessions of the Evangelical Lutheran Church*, ed. Robert Kolb and Timothy J. Wengert, trans. Charles P. Arand (Minneapolis: Augsburg Fortress, 2000), 34.

[5] Hank Voss helpfully summarizes this material in *The Priesthood of All Believers and the Missio Dei* (Eugene, OR: Pickwick, 2016).

[6] In this essay, lowercase "word" refers to Scripture, and uppercase "Word" refers to the divine Son.

writer and adviser in heaven and on earth. That is why his words can have no more than the one simplest meaning which we call the written one, or the literal meaning."[7]

Luther thought that ministers were simply in place to guide hearers to reflect on God's word. Their messages should begin with the preaching of the law, holding up God's divine requirements and the reality of sin and judgment. It was at this point that Luther believed the consolation of the gospel could bring relief. Then, when Christ was preached, the Spirit would awaken in each believer the need for repentance. Greater contemplation of the word would produce contrition and, ultimately, a sense of forgiveness and rebirth by the Spirit.[8]

Accordingly, Luther and the Reformers rejected the papal tradition—for the biblical text "interprets itself"; believers need only listen with a heart open to the Spirit's transforming proclamation issued through the gospel message. We can, nevertheless, find Luther grappling with the partial obscurity of Scripture's meanings in his 1528 preface to Isaiah, where he lists foundational rules for accessing the text's clear content. Among these, he includes the "rule of faith," the hermeneutic principle maintaining that the passages of Scripture which set forth gospel teaching with the greatest clarity should be used to interpret the passages that may be less clear. Hence, because Luther took the message of *sola gratia* (salvation through grace alone) to be the heart of the gospel proclamation, he set the "salvation by faith" Pauline texts over the "salvation by works" texts, such as Hebrews and James, in terms of their primacy for interpreting other parts of Scripture.

[7] Martin Luther, "Concerning the Letter and the Spirit," in *Luther's Works*, American ed., vol. 39, ed. Jaroslav Pelikan and Helmut Lehman (St. Louis: Concordia, 1958–1986), 178.

[8] For more on Luther's understanding of the Spirit in the life of a believer, see Pekka A. Kärkkäinen, "Luther's Theological Psychology and the Spirit," *Lutherjahrbuch* 85 (2018): 154–71.

Assessing the Early Protestant View

Luther has been critiqued for never working out with methodological diligence the procedural norms for identifying and applying the "rule of faith." His silence on this point is, indeed, somewhat puzzling, given his critique of the "uncertain opinions" of church teachers. Roman Catholic theologian Louis Bouyer has suggested that Luther's oversight may be the correlate of the fact that "it was a living intuition of salvation that crystallised his view of the Bible" rather than the reverse.[9] Bouyer's suggestion makes sense. Luther believed that, in encountering the proclaimed gospel, one fundamentally encounters the message of *sola gratia*. In that encounter, one is shown that grace could never be accessed through righteous works mandated by an ecclesiastical leadership or infused via reception of the sacraments; rather, grace may only be received via the unmerited gift of faith, provided by God through Christ crucified. The content of this realization then constitutes the self-interpreting norm of the Bible's coherent content. The point is, for Luther, a living intuition of salvation crystallizes the view of Scripture, rather than the reverse.

Here lie the roots of *sola scriptura*'s ill-fated future: Luther and his followers took the Bible's concentration of meaning to be in need only of something like commonsense recognition, rather than a communal definition. As Wolfhart Pannenberg suggests, their operative notion of commonsense perception was funded by the belief that only the "light of the universal judgment of reason" is needed to see the manifest facts of Scripture's content, and the Holy Spirit provides the "inner clarity" of Scripture's spiritual meanings.[10] One could argue that this sensibility is the point from which

---

[9] Louis Bouyer, *The Spirit and Forms of Protestantism*, trans. A. V. Littledale (Westminster, MD: Newman, 1957), 116–17.

[10] Wolfhart Pannenberg, *Basic Questions in Theology: Collected Essays*, trans. George H. Kehm (Philadelphia: Fortress, 1970), 1:63.

Protestantism's defining strength emerges—its remarkable history of encouraging in believers an enlivening "biblical spirituality," to echo Bouyer's analysis again. In other words, Protestant believers have traditionally engaged in a living spiritual practice of constant return to Scripture as a source of life-giving, personal contact with God. Across time and space, this practice has elicited trust in and testament to the Holy Spirit's illumination continually taking the expressive forms it needs. Informed by this laudable spiritual disposition, Bouyer says, the church is rightly recognized as the people "whom [God] does not cease to call and fashion, breathing into it the breath of his mouth."[11]

Arguably, then, on the one hand, this undergirding feature of the Reformers' turn to "Scripture alone" is something that today's Protestants should work to retain. On the other hand, they should still seek to purge away the unsustainable features of the *sola scriptura* heritage. Those unsustainable features are evidenced by the unfolding history of Protestantism. As *sola scriptura* adherents followed the new hermeneutical program beyond the advent of the Reformation, they enjoyed the freedom of individual responsibility for scriptural interpretation. But an unnamed politics held sway in their corporate gatherings around magnetic leaders such as Luther, Calvin, and Zwingli. That politics became volatile, not least because the Reformers' agreement upon Scripture's theological meaning relied upon intuition and commonsense agreement. As commonsense perception began to shift, Protestants had no doctrinal basis for drawing upon church tradition to relieve the tensions arising from scriptural exposition. Though they carried forth traditional practices of convening synods and composing confessions, such conventions bore no sacred weight in the minds of their dissenters.

[11] Bouyer, *Spirit and Forms of Protestantism*, 124.

Later Protestant Approaches to Biblical Authority

The post-Reformation period of the seventeenth century saw significant advances in astronomy, physics, and mathematics, ushering in the so-called Scientific Revolution. In a departure from Luther's work, the rationalists of the day, such as Francis Bacon and René Descartes, questioned the a priori starting point of the Bible's authority. Rather, they declared reflective reason to be the reliable norm for human convictions and stressed the "reasonable" aspects of Christianity as the standards for scriptural interpretation. By the end of the Enlightenment, biblical interpretation and theological reasoning came to focus on the pressing question of whether or not humanity had evolved beyond the need for religious institutions. Special revelation was more or less subsumed under the pronouncements of scientific historical research, which was taken to be infallible both as a method in its own right and as a means for accounting for the reality of faith. The divide between scholarship and faith solidified further as biblical interpretation underwent this "turn to history." Historicist investigation became the dominant framework for biblical understanding, resulting in interpretive quests such as Albert Schweitzer's search for the historical Jesus.

A remarkable challenge to this trajectory in academic theology appeared when the so-called Neo-Orthodox movement arose in Europe. Reformed theologian Karl Barth became Neo-Orthodoxy's prolific voice when he published his commentary on Romans (1919). Like Luther, Barth found God speaking through Paul directly into Barth's own historical situation. In that experience, Barth and his associates discovered God as "Wholly Other," evoking the crisis of all natural theological methods and philosophical apologetics. As a result, they advocated a rather astonishing recovery of Protestant "word of God" theology for the modern era.

In his commentary on Romans, Barth provocatively asserted that if he "had to choose" between the modern historical-critical method and "the old doctrine of inspiration," he would "resolutely choose the latter."[12] Yet it was not his intent to shun historical-critical work in favor of reverting to a precritical view of Scripture's literal historicity. In championing the old Protestant doctrine of inspiration over the modern historical reading of Scripture, Barth simply intended to reject the dominance of scientific-historical critique in biblical exegesis, on the grounds that this dominance issued from a short-sighted historicism. Barth specifically maintained that historical scholars were not *self*-critical enough.[13] They had overlooked the fact that the key to understanding a text, including the Bible, "must be sought from the text itself, and moreover from its spirit, content and aim."[14] By setting up their science as an absolute reading of Scripture, the historical critics had fallen short of attending to what the divine subject of Scripture demands from its audience: submission.[15] Moreover, like Luther, Barth maintained that our faith response to the gospel "is not a determination of human action which man can give to it at will or maintain at will once it is received." Rather, that response is itself a gift afforded by "the gracious address of God to man, the free personal presence of Jesus Christ in his activity."[16]

Barth accordingly identified anchor points for proper theological hermeneutics issuing from two Christological principles. First, he argued, theologians must begin with the question, What is the word of God? And if they heed the declaration of John 1:1

[12] Karl Barth, *The Epistle to the Romans*, trans. Edwyn C. Hoskyns (London: Oxford University Press, 1968).

[13] Barth, *Epistle to the Romans*, 2–15.

[14] Barth, *Epistle to the Romans*, 108.

[15] Cf. Barth, *Epistle to the Romans*, 8; see also Karl Barth, *Church Dogmatics*, ed. Frank McCombie, trans. G. W. Bromley and T. F. Torrance, 31 vols. (London: T&T Clark, 2009), 1.2:458.

[16] Barth, *Church Dogmatics*, 1.2:466, 469.

(NRSV)—"In the beginning was the Word, and the Word was with God, and the Word was God"—then they should understand God's word not primarily as some sort of content, but as the living act whereby God comes to us through Christ's personal presence. God's word is, after all, fundamentally something that *occurs*—an event whereby God takes hold of us.

Second, Barth took the miraculous twofold nature of Christ's full humanity and divinity as disclosing the fact that divine self-revelation in the creaturely sphere does not entail God's "tapping into" some unique nature or capacity we possess. Rather, revelation will always have the character of the inexplicable, coming entirely from beyond us. The material means of revelation—including nature, history, and even the words of the Bible—mediate God's word only because God freely utilizes them to become personally present to the human audience, with perception-transforming results. Such encounters remain irreconcilable with any general process of human analysis.

Assessing Barth's Views

A key difference between Barth's "Word of God" theology and Luther's rests on the fact that Luther did not see any significant distance between God's Word and human words when the latter is inspired by the Holy Spirit. For Barth, on the other hand, the distance between God's Word and our words cannot be overcome. The human expressions constituting Scripture's testimony and the church's proclamation are no different from any other creaturely phenomena in terms of their potential for fostering God's communion with humanity, in other words; God alone brings this about. The distance between God's Word and our experiential understanding, however, can be *bridged* by the miraculous gift of the Spirit. By the Spirit's presence, we experience ourselves opening to God's Word through faith-evoking revelation. When Scripture functions as revelatory, it is because God has assigned the linguistic medium as the means whereby the word should thus grasp the interpreter's mind, providing a transformed vision. Via the Bible, believers experience the death of ordinary meaning, resurrected in the form of a concrete portrait of Christ.

Barth thus accounts for the human interpreter's subjective experience and expression by asserting that human witness and response to revelation remain humanly limited, but the believer's faith response to the divine address is nevertheless assured by the personal presence of God in that address. In this manner, Barth brilliantly grappled with the modern crisis of the Bible's historical meaningfulness by asserting that the question of the Bible's meaning cannot be properly articulated via principles formulated independently of our being grasped by God. Barth thereby called biblical interpreters to begin not by reflecting theoretically upon human appropriation of the revelatory artifact but in an act of spiritual submission—that is, by seeking correspondence to God's living Word by submitting to being interpreted by *it*.[17] Only in the midst of that ongoing submission may the interpreter authentically begin the work of theology—that is, the work of suggesting how God's Word stands in relation to historical realities.

Barth's project stands as a kind of modern *sola scriptura* option in two respects. First, it calls for submission to the Bible's distinctive mandates in relation to God, its supreme subject. Second, Barth's project effectively wrests the meaning of revelation away from the modern-day intellectual hierarchy by envisioning Scripture's theological meaning as the gift given by the Spirit to any believer who sincerely seeks God's will. In contrast with Luther's approach and its need for common agreement regarding Scripture's doctrinal content, Barth's hermeneutic paradigm helpfully anticipates the reality of interpretive discrepancies among believers. Such signs of human limitation are, for Barth, woven into our testament to

[17] See Barth, *Church Dogmatics*, 1.1:295–96.

the impossible possibility of God's speaking to us. They are even a key feature of the historical occasion of revelation, pressing us to listen for how God is speaking in our present situations.

There is, however, a problematic sense whereby Barth's hermeneutic approach reiterates Luther's *sola scriptura* endeavor. In both of their projects, we find a version of the same circular argument at play. The Bible attests that receiving God's word via the grace of the Spirit's action provokes a decision of faith, and only on the basis of that extrinsic gift can the reader engage in faithful scriptural interpretation. It is not necessarily circular to suggest that satisfactory biblical interpretation is only possible once the interpreter has submitted to the spiritual mode of existence and that the Bible's content somehow attests to that principle. The circularity resides in one's asserting that God *extrinsically* provides the vision of revelation that one presents—that is, in a manner that cannot be assessed by the discursive community. As Werner Jeanrond describes, what was "'justification by faith' for Luther, is 'God's otherness' (yet closeness) for Barth."[18] On both accounts, the Spirit provides Scripture's meaningful concentration through grace that works upon us rather than cooperating with our efforts.

And so, for all of its remarkable achievements, it seems that Barth's hermeneutic approach does not finally overcome the limitation that has beleaguered the history of *sola scriptura*: *sola scriptura* has tended to present the gospel's content as if it requires intuitive recognition, rather than definition, to be perceived. Within these parameters, the interpreter turns forever inward, taking his or her personal, spiritual experience of the word as the touchstone for theological disclosure, with little ability to conceive of bodily contexts (corporate or corporeal) as crucial sites of divine self-disclosure.

[18] Jeanrond, *Theological Hermeneutics*, 130.

Exemplary Moves beyond Barth: Wolfhart Pannenberg and Hans Frei

There has been no shortage of thoughtful, critical responses to Barth's hermeneutic project from Protestant quarters. Prominent among these responders are, for instance, two theological giants: Wolfhart Pannenberg and Hans Frei. Both thinkers worked to eschew any tendency (like Barth's) to suppose that there are "intrinsic limits between a realm of supernatural knowledge and a contrasting realm of so-called natural knowledge," as Pannenberg puts it.[19]

To this end, Pannenberg emphasizes historical consciousness, arguing that the very possibility of such consciousness lies in the realm of the theological—namely, in the Hebraic conception of God's relation to creation (which fundamentally entails the concept that God moves events in time toward a future fulfillment). From this perspective, full revelation occurs only at history's conclusion, at which point one may finally discern the total "framework of the history which God has with humanity and through humanity with his whole creation."[20] Christian witness attests that this eschatological totality has been disclosed proleptically in Christ's resurrection. Hence, for Christian theology, the fullness of revelation is both "moving toward a future still hidden from the world" *and* already anticipated in Jesus's fate.[21] Pannenberg thus envisions the endeavor of Christian theology to "tak[e] every thought captive into the obedience of Christ" not as involving some dialectical death-and-resurrection movement from secular to sacred content, as he suggests Barth implies.[22] Instead, we can only understand the universal history and significance of Scripture's testimony in light of each other.

[19] Pannenberg, *Basic Questions*, 1:13.
[20] Pannenberg, *Basic Questions*, 1:15.
[21] Pannenberg, *Basic Questions*, 1:15.
[22] Pannenberg, *Basic Questions*, 1:13–14.

Frei similarly worried that Barth's approach to revelation indicates that history is like an empty container that can be discarded once the revelatory encounter with God in Christ has occurred. He was convinced that this cannot be the case because, for instance, it is of utmost importance that we frame Jesus as a first-century Jew to understand the import of his message and ministry. Frei thus sought to conceive of Christomorphic revelation as compatible with structures of human meaning and discernment, while also recognizing this revelation's transformative potency and its interpreters as ineradicably historically situated. In that process, he worked out an ad hoc approach to theological discernment—one rooted in confidence that the New Testament portrait of Christ can transform the human imagination, impacting every site of meaning making. For Frei, this significance unfolds over time as the Holy Spirit empowers faithful, submissive Christian interpretation, mediating between human sociocultural expression and the unfolding of Christocentric revelation.[23]

Projects such as Pannenberg's and Frei's represent useful Protestant alternatives to Barth's revisioning of *sola scriptura*, given that they powerfully present the gospel's core meaning as requiring definition, rather than intuitive recognition, to be perceived. More specifically, they manage to frame theological interpretation as an ongoing process that occurs via the corporate body's dialogical processes, and they do so without espousing a hierarchy of teaching office. On close examination, however, one could argue that there remain problematic aspects to their approaches—particularly concerning the role they allow the *corporeal* body in perceiving revelation. In articulating his vision for corporate theological discernment, Pannenberg effectively subordinates the imaginative and affective features of faith perception—along

[23] See Paul DeHart, *The Trial of the Witnesses: The Rise and Decline of Postliberal Theology* (Malden, MA: Blackwell, 2006), 257–59.

with the Bible's literary import—to a rationalist account of the universal significance of the Christ event. Frei gives fruitful attention to Scripture's literary features, but he does not satisfactorily account for our practical access points for attending to the Spirit's promptings.

Of course, Pannenberg's and Frei's post-Barthian approaches to Scripture hardly represent all contemporary Protestant hermeneutic projects. I take specific interest in them here simply because they stand among its giants and because they represent two influential options on its landscape: Pannenberg supported systematic theology as a post-Enlightenment, interdisciplinary science; his work has thus called us to resist withdrawing into ecclesial enclaves, imagining stark divides between spheres of religious and secular discourse. Frei served as a progenitor of the so-called postliberal school of theology, which has taught us to attend to the role of the biblical metanarrative in shaping Christian grammar and practice. And yet—either by oversimplifying or too quickly bracketing off various existential drives that compel readers to engage the biblical witness as normative—their approaches may encourage us to *pursue* Scripture's theological content without suitably accounting for our subjective involvement in *shaping* or *discerning* that theological content.

In sum, though we have gained much from the accomplishments of such projects, we can see that Protestant readers remain at a loss in the face of the subjectivity of theological interpretation. It seems that the "priesthood of all believers," as an interpretive community, needs to take theological stock of the content of Christian confession *and* of the subjective experience that produces confession—that is, of the desires and drives that the Spirit appropriates in the graced unfolding of God's mission in the world. On these grounds, the Protestant conundrum may beg for what systematic theologian Sarah Coakley calls "a contemplative alternative" to "theological stuckness in the knowing subject."[24]

Risking Response to God: Toward Application

Having surveyed the hermeneutic routes our Protestant forbears have taken, it seems fitting that we now set our sights on paths beyond *sola scriptura*, as it were. We do so with confidence in the Spirit to continually enable our conception of God's word, breathing into it new life in every interpretive situation. We can find paradigms for paths beyond *sola scriptura* in Scripture itself, particularly in passages that speak to the mingling of divine and human desires.

The Bible is filled with images of God desiring intimacy with God's people, readily making use of analogies of wooing and nuptial union toward that end. In Isaiah 49:14–15, we find the image of maternal longing standing as another scriptural site wherein physical longing for an "other" functions as an analogy for God's desire for God's people: "But Zion said, 'The LORD has forsaken me, my Lord has forgotten me.' Can a woman forget her nursing child, or show no compassion for the child of her womb? Even these may forget, yet I will not forget you" (NRSV). This image of God longing for us as a nursing mother aches to feed her infant is rich with pneumatological implications.

In the interest of drawing them out, we might consider a reflection on the mother's experience of nursing, which Bonnie Miller-McLemore describes as follows:

> As with pregnancy, lactation subverts artificial boundaries between self and other, inside and outside. Both undermine the integrity of my body and my self, and root me fluidly, solidly, to the depths of my body's

[24] Sarah Coakley, *God, Sexuality, and the Self: An Essay "On the Trinity"* (Cambridge: Cambridge University Press, 2013), 75.

> capacities. . . . I know by an affective connection that moves toward differentiation, not by comparison, contrast, and critique or by some idealized oneness or union with the child.[25]

Miller-McLemore's description of the bond between a nursing mother and child tunes our ears to hear pneumatological echoes in Isaiah's picture of divine, maternal desire—that is, this image discloses the ontological boundaries between ourselves and God as transgressed, but not destroyed, by "an affective connection that moves toward differentiation." In the terms of the Christian tradition, such a connection between Creator and creature is afforded by the Spirit's indwelling of creation, infusing it with eschatological hope of relational union.

Coakley highlights this feature of the Spirit's work by focusing on the prayer experience attested in Romans 8. She reads this passage as disclosing that there is "an inherent reflexivity in the divine, a ceaseless outgoing and return of the desiring God," which is the Holy Spirit itself, and significantly, "it is this 'reflexivity in God,' this Holy Spirit, that makes incarnate life possible."[25] That is to say, the pneumatology of Romans indicates that the Spirit is "that without which there would be no incarnated Son at all, and—by extension—no life of Sonship into which we, too, might enter by participation."[27] Pursuing this theme, Coakley here finds further implications that

> the life of "Sonship" . . . is not only not restricted to Jesus's human (male) life, but nor to the mystical "body of Christ" which is the church; it is in this passage expanded even further to include the full

[25] Bonnie J. Miller-McLemore, *Also a Mother: Work and Family as Theological Dilemma* (Nashville: Abingdon, 1994), 147.

[26] Coakley, *God, Sexuality, and the Self*, 56.

[27] Coakley, *God, Sexuality, and the Self*, 56.

> cosmological implications of the incarnation, the whole creation "groaning" to its final Christological telos in God (Romans 8:18–21). What this underscores is the extraordinary ripple effect of prayer in the Spirit—its inexorably social and even cosmic significance as an act of cooperation with, and incorporation into, the still extending life of the incarnation.[28]

Coakley thus understands the incorporative Spirit as evoking ecstatic response to God. The whole creation "groans" in the Spirit toward its Christological telos, and believers are incorporated into the "still extending life of the incarnation" as they labor with and for the world. Hence, as the Spirit works to bestow on creation the Christomorphic shape of God's love, that bestowal means that the life of the Son—and, with it, revelation itself—is still unfolding, agonistically, in the cosmic expanse of history.

Situated in light of this framing of pneumatological incorporation, the fact that efforts to secure a risk-free approach to biblical interpretation have proven futile is a reality with transcendent implications. The upshot is that it is not in "getting it right" that we discover the Spirit-infused, graced nature of the communicative encounter with God. Drawing upon Rowan Williams, we may say that

> grace, for the Christian believer, is a transformation that depends in large part on knowing yourself to be seen in a certain way: as significant, as wanted. The whole story of creation, incarnation, and our incorporation into the fellowship of Christ's body tells us that God desires us, *as if we were God*, as if we were that unconditional response to God's giving that God's self makes in the life of the Trinity. We are created so that we may be caught

[28] Coakley, *God, Sexuality, and the Self*, 114.

> up in this, so that we may grow into the wholehearted love of God by learning that God loves us as God loves God.[29]

Coakley and Williams both offer pictures of the God–world relation wherein God's self-disclosure occurs in a manner that wants to be received, enjoyed, and even reconstructed by the perception of others. God desires us as a speaker longs to be heard by an addressee—not by an empty echo chamber, capable of neatly reproducing that speech, but by one who receives the word *into* and responds to it *out of* his or her distinctive otherness; one who longs to be heard in turn, finding in God's responsive presence an occasion of joy. We might say that, in the Holy Spirit's mission to mediate God's self-expression, the Spirit invokes creaturely "collaboration" in determining the word's material life.

Among myriad implications, these tenets of a Spirit-led approach to revelation mean that we ought not indulge the longing to interpret Scripture from a neutral, invulnerable standpoint, without "getting a few fingers caught" in the act.[30] We invite the transfiguring guidance of the Holy Spirit when instead we root our interpretation in impassioned, self-offering attention to the divine Other whom we encounter through the text. But what happens when believers' respective readings of the word clash and become a source of conflict?

On this point, Protestant readers can begin by echoing Luther's affirmation that the individual's apprehension of the divine word in Scripture is given via the Holy Spirit's witness to faith, which is an unmerited gift of grace. We should go on, however, to complicate any "commonsense" hermeneutic presumptions by specifying

[29] Rowan D. Williams, "The Body's Grace," in *Theology and Sexuality: Classic and Contemporary Readings*, ed. Eugene F. Rogers Jr. (Oxford: Blackwell, 2002), 311–12; italics original.

[30] Cf. Jacques Derrida, *Dissemination*, trans. Barbara Johnson (Chicago: University of Chicago Press, 1981), 63.

that the incorporative Spirit affords apprehension while also evoking human interpretive collaboration in shaping the Word's meanings. That collaborative process is one we must recognize as occurring on "both sides" of the biblical text, as it were—first among the composing, canonizing community, and later among us, the reading community of faith.

Discerning the "inspired" meaning of mediated revelation is, then, an indelibly *bodily* activity—in the corporeal, corporate, and textual senses of the word. It warrants as full an awareness as possible of the material, communal, and intertextual situations out of which the text in question arises and into which it speaks. Such an awareness must include the data afforded by historical-critical investigation, but it cannot stop there. It should recover the interpretive body's *spirituality* by moving toward the embrace of multiple means of "knowing," with its adherents becoming vulnerable to "getting a few fingers caught" in the process of identifying the Christomorphic meaning of the text that emerges out of and seeps into the community's shared life. Such a picture calls to mind not a passively receptive audience but co-laborers with the Spirit, filled with longing akin to Paul's in seeking to interpret the gospel for the Galatians—those for whom he found himself "in the pain of childbirth until Christ is formed in you" (Gal. 4:19 NRSV).

There is a cue here for imagining the believing community's interpretive endeavor as a kind of "maternal" one. This analogy could help us consider the nature of our hermeneutic enterprise by illuminating the nature of fervent and often belabored attention to the desired "object." For the mother, this object is the flourishing of the child; for the church, it is the emergence of the Christomorphic interpretation that the church seeks to discern. Both the mother and the church, in this analogy, share a "maternal knowing." As Miller-McLemore describes it, maternal knowing must

> rely upon a bodily passion, a knowing driven by a welcomed lust or need that seeks satisfaction. . . . In this state, I learn, change, and develop; if I don't, the child won't. . . . Very few abstracted rules hold. In the movement between the knowing and the acting of nursing and tending an infant, I use a mode of circular reasoning, interweaving physical sensation, momentary cognition, behavioral reaction, and a physical sensing and intellectual reading of the results—a trial and error, hit-and-miss strategy.[31]

Here we see that the mother's involvement in the interpretive process does not arise from a passive reception of meaning but from her intense desire for the child's life. The mother deploys various forms of deciphering the situation, identifying and responding to its shifting demands so as to sustain the child's life.

This picture of "maternal discernment" can, I propose, provide an analogy for how the Spirit-led church body may deploy multiple means of knowing in the enterprise of scriptural interpretation. One could begin by drawing upon this analogy to suggest that the praying community ("the mother") should expect to labor continually in delineating and responding effectively to this desired but often mystifying object of devotion: the Christomorphic meaning of the text ("the child"). This process requires painstaking discernment, rather than commonsense reading. The body's members must put all of their knowing powers to work in interpreting the text under consideration, ever seeking the Christomorphic shape and implications of that text for the community's present historical situation.

There is precedent for such a communal process of hermeneutic discernment in key moments in Scripture, a primary one being the inclusion of Gentiles in the family of God. Luke Timothy

[31] Miller-McLemore, *Also a Mother*, 147.

Johnson points out how, in the Acts 15 account of the Apostolic Council's discernment process, we see the church "deciding its future" as God's people via a theological process.[32] That process is oriented *by* communal reflection upon Scripture (i.e., the story of God's mighty acts with Israel), the words of Jesus, and the Holy Spirit's apparent promptings via Peter's experiences culminating with Cornelius's conversion. The process is oriented toward practice. The community's decision does not involve a tidy or quick procedure, but rather "involv[es] many believers in many places, and the decisions of many local communities," Johnson points out. He continues,

> The experiences of diverse people and the narrative of those experiences—in an ever-widening circle—provide the primary theological data. As those who testify speak of their experience of God, so do those who listen weigh what is said: They exercise discernment. The people who have these experiences, moreover, are people already attentive to the Lord in prayer, and thus open to the new and surprising ways God might act, both in their own and in others' lives. . . . The words of Jesus and the Scriptures are normative for the believers, but in a way that allows new and deeper understanding of them. Throughout these accounts, the experience of God's activity stimulates the church to reread the Scriptures and to discover ever new ways in which God maintains continuity with Godself [*sic*].[33]

Framing the early church's process in the terms of the maternal epistemic paradigm, we find that we ought not expect to find a surefire methodological formula or hierarchy of knowledge when

---

[32] Luke Timothy Johnson, *Scripture and Discernment: Decision Making in the Church* (Nashville: Abingdon, 1996), 106.

[33] Johnson, *Scripture and Discernment*, 107.

discerning Scripture's Christomorphic meanings. Rather, we are fundamentally called into a certain prayerful *posture*—one oriented toward the pursuit of the identity of God disclosed to us in the biblical story of God with us, one eager to be formed in that God's holy likeness, and one open to the possibility of surprise when relying upon the Spirit's guidance.[34]

In that posture, we must be ready to deploy something akin to a trial-and-error, hit-or-miss strategy as we prayerfully and creatively draw upon the full range of the body's modes of perception in discovering how God is maintaining continuity with God's own self. Playing upon Miller-McLemore's terms provided previously, we could say that our strategy will make use of the body's gifts for "momentary cognition," afforded by the intuition of sanctified disciples; "behavioral reaction," cultured by a lifelong devotion to Christomorphic kenosis; "physical sensing," acquired by occupying the margins of discursive privilege; and "intellectual reading of the results," developed through careful exegetical and theological investigation. The "members" of this body should not be considered as only those available to us locally. While this effort will, of course, always begin in the local body of believers, it should expand to attend to the voices of members of Christ's body well beyond the bounds of one's local context geographically, historically, and even denominationally.

In the midst of this process, we are called to trust the communal body's grace: to believe that the Spirit cooperates with the discursive community that is bent on seeking Christomorphic life and is willing to admit its need for forgiveness and maturation. This means giving credence to hard-won doctrinal consensus—at least provisionally. Simultaneously, careful attention to the Spirit's promptings indicates that subverting established orders and

[34] I am also inspired by John Mark Hicks's convincing arguments to this effect in *Searching for the Pattern: My Journey in Interpreting the Bible* (John Mark Hicks, 2019). See especially parts 2 and 3.

systems of belief is often bound up with heeding the other-oriented call of divine desire. This is evidenced in the Romans 8 prayer experience noted previously. Here we find that incorporation into Sonship occurs at the cost of vulnerability to the Holy Spirit's interruption, so as to progress in the joy of authentic attention to God and one another. This highlights the enduring need for Spirit-beseeching contemplative practice, and as Acts 15 reminds us, such practice "will always stand at the edges of institutional acceptability, always be pressing to an 'orthodoxy' beyond mere propositional assent," to borrow Coakley's phrasing.[35] The emergent forms of doctrine and institutional order must, in other words, be eschatologically oriented, held as points for ongoing re-engagement—particularly from the vantage point of previously unheard discursive partners, both within and beyond the associations of church discourse. The hermeneutic of trust should turn a scrupulous eye to the mainstays of power within ecclesial bodies, continually asking how its agents are accountable to the body and the call into God's future.

Protestants are a highly diverse group of people, united by both our failures and our extraordinary trust in and witness to the Spirit's guidance as we turn, time and again, to Scripture: our source of life-giving, personal contact with God. In the end, I have simply argued that it is high time we pay closer attention to what is actually happening in that process, so that we might leave behind the unsustainable (and unfaithful) features of our hermeneutic traditions. And I have recommended our turning to the intersections of spirituality and theology as a resource for future hermeneutic practice, but with the caveat that we are cautious in doing so: we must take measures to ensure that this turning does not become a new means of supposing that we have control over the God-breathed implications of Scripture. I believe something

---

[35] Coakley, *God, Sexuality, and the Self*, 341–42.

like a "maternal paradigm" of the church's discernment process finally reminds us that the challenge of ongoing communal negotiation with Scripture—of truly listening for the voice of God speaking to us through the text and of listening to one another vis-à-vis our wrestling with the implications of the text—is not to be underestimated. Yet Christ's assurance of the Spirit's presence in our midst also promises that, in our labors to discover Scripture's Christomorphic meanings together over time, we can learn that the struggles which produced scriptural testimony and canonization—and which still produce its interpretation—are themselves occasions of transfiguration: sites wherein the Spirit shapes us for the moves of Sonship and thus for faithfully apprehending the Word within words.

Selected Bibliography

Aberbach, Moses, and Leivy Smolar. "Aaron, Jeroboam and the Golden Calves," *Journal of Biblical Literature* 86 (1967): 129–40.

Armour, Ellen T. *Deconstruction, Feminist Theology, and the Problem of Difference: Subverting the Race/Gender Divide*. Chicago: University of Chicago Press, 1999.

Augustine of Hippo. *The City of God against the Pagans*. Translated and edited by R. W. Dyson. Cambridge: Cambridge University Press, 1998.

Balthasar, Hans Urs von. *Glory of the Lord*. 2nd ed. Translated by Erasmo Leiva-Merikakis. San Francisco: Ignatius, 2009.

Barrett, C. K. *The First Epistle to the Corinthians*. Black's New Testament Commentary. London: Continuum, 1968.

Barth, Karl. *Church Dogmatics*. 31 vols. 1961. Translated by G. W. Bromley and T. F. Torrance. London: T&T Clark, 2009.

———. *The Epistle to the Romans*. Edited by Frank McCombie. Translated by Edwyn C. Hoskyns. London: Oxford University Press, 1968.

Bates, Matthew W. *The Hermeneutics of the Apostolic Proclamation: The Center of Paul's Method of Scriptural Interpretation*. Waco, TX: Baylor University Press, 2012.

Bauer, Walter. *Orthodoxy and Heresy in Earliest Christianity*. Edited by Robert A. Kraft and Gerhard Krodel. Philadelphia: Fortress, 1971.

Bauer, Walter, William Arndt, F. Wilbur Gingrich, and Frederick W. Danker, eds. *A Greek-English Lexicon of the New Testament and Other Early Christian Literature*. Translated by Frederick W. Danker. 3rd ed. Chicago: University of Chicago Press, 2000.

Bendavid, Abba. *Parallels in the Bible*. Jerusalem: Carta, 1965.

Bettenson, Henry, and Chris Maunder, eds. *Documents of the Christian Church*. 4th ed. London: Oxford University Press, 2011.
Blass, Friedrich, Albert Debrunner, and Robert Walter Funk. *A Greek Grammar of the New Testament and Other Early Christian Literature*. Chicago: University of Chicago Press, 1961.
Boda, Mark. *The Heartbeat of Old Testament Theology: Three Creedal Expressions*. Grand Rapids: Baker Academic, 2017.
Bogard, Ben, ed. *Pillars of Orthodoxy, or Defenders of the Faith*. Louisville: Baptist Book Concern, 1900.
Bokedal, Tomas. "The Rule of Faith: Tracing Its Origins." *Journal of Theological Interpretation* 7 (2013): 233–55.
Bonhoeffer, Dietrich. *The Cost of Discipleship*. Edited by Irmgard Booth. Translated by R. H. Fuller. Rev. ed. New York: Macmillan, 1963.
Boring, M. Eugene. *Disciples and the Bible: A History of Disciples Biblical Interpretation in North America*. St. Louis: Chalice Press, 1997.
Bosnan, J. P. "The Paradoxical Presence of Exodus 34:6–7 in the Book of the Twelve." *Scriptura* 87 (2004): 233–43.
Bouyer, Louis. *The Spirit and Forms of Protestantism*. Translated by A. V. Littledale. Westminster, MD: Newman, 1957.
Bowden, Henry Warner. "Perplexity over a Protean Principle: A Response." In *The American Quest for the Primitive Church*, edited by Richard T. Hughes, 171–78. Chicago: University of Illinois Press, 1988.
Brents, T. W. *The Gospel Plan of Salvation*. Nashville: Gospel Advocate, 1874.
Bullinger, Heinrich. *De Origine Erroris*. Zurich: In Officina Froschoviana, Mense Martio, 1539. Accessed September 16, 2019, https://doi.org/10.3931/e-rara-2603.
Cameron, Euan. "Primitivism, Patristics, and Polemic in Protestant Visions of Early Christianity." In *Sacred History: Uses of the Christian Past in the Renaissance World*, edited by Katherine Van Liere, Simon Ditchfield, and Howard Louthan, 27–51. Oxford: Oxford University Press, 2012.
Campbell, Alexander. "Address to the Public." *Christian Baptist* 2 (1824): 33–42.
———. "The Bible—Principles of Interpretation." *Millennial Harbinger* 3, no. 1 (1846): 13–24.

———. "Campbellism Examined." *Millennial Harbinger* 4, no. 5 (1855): 61–75.

———. "Reply." *Christian Baptist* 5 (1827): 208–11.

Campbell, Alexander, and John B. Purcell. *A Debate on the Roman Catholic Religion*. Cincinnati: Benziger, 1837.

Campbell, Thomas. "Declaration and Address." In *The Quest for Christian Unity, Peace, and Purity in Thomas Campbell's* Declaration and Address: *Text and Studies*, edited by Thomas H. Olbricht and Hans Rollmann, 3–58. ATLA Monograph Series 46. Lanham, MD: Scarecrow, 2000.

Carr, David M. *Writing on the Tablet of the Heart: Origins of Scripture and Literature*. Oxford: Oxford University Press, 2008.

Cary, Jeffrey. *Free Churches and the Body of Christ: Authority, Unity, and Truthfulness*. Eugene, OR: Cascade, 2012.

Chadwick, Owen. *From Bossuet to Newman*. 2nd ed. Cambridge: Cambridge University Press, 1987.

Chesterton, Gilbert K. *What's Wrong with the World*. New York: Dodd, Mead & Company, 1910.

Childs, Brevard S. *Biblical Theology in Crisis*. Philadelphia: Westminster, 1970.

———. *The Book of Exodus: A Critical, Theological Commentary*. Old Testament Library. Philadelphia: Westminster John Knox Press, 1974.

Ciampa, Roy E., and Brian S. Rosner. *The First Letter to the Corinthians*. Pillar New Testament Commentary. Grand Rapids: Eerdmans, 2010.

Coakley, Sarah. *God, Sexuality, and the Self: An Essay "On the Trinity."* Cambridge: Cambridge University Press, 2013.

Conzelmann, Hans. *1 Corinthians: A Commentary on the First Epistle to the Corinthians*. Translated by James W. Leitch. Hermeneia. Philadelphia: Fortress, 1975.

Cornwall, Robert D. "Christology." In *Encyclopedia of the Stone-Campbell Movement*, edited by Paul M. Blowers, Anthony L. Dunnavant, Douglas A. Foster, and D. Newell Williams, 204–5. Grand Rapids: Eerdmans, 2004.

Decker, William B. "Baptismal Confession." *Restoration Quarterly* 1 (1957): 180–84.

DeHart, Paul. *The Trial of the Witnesses: The Rise and Decline of Postliberal Theology*. Malden, MA: Blackwell, 2006.

Derrida, Jacques. *Dissemination*. Translated by Barbara Johnson. Chicago: University of Chicago Press, 1981.

Dix, Gregory, and Henry Chadwick, eds. *The Treatise on the Apostolic Tradition of St. Hippolytus of Rome, Bishop and Martyr*. London: Alban Press, 1992.

Dobbs-Allsopp, F. W., J. J. M. Roberts, C. J. Seow, and R. E. Whitaker, eds. *Hebrew Inscriptions: Texts from the Biblical Period of the Monarchy with Concordance*. New Haven, CT: Yale University Press, 2005.

Dungan, D. R. *Hermeneutics: A Text-Book*. 2nd ed. Cincinnati: Standard, 1888.

Eliot, T. S. *Collected Poems 1909–1962*. London: Faber, 1974.

Elliger, Karl, and Wilhelm Rudolph, eds. *Biblia Hebraica Stuttgartensia*. 5th rev. ed. prepared by Adrian Schenker. Stuttgart: Deutsche Bibelgesellschaft, 1997.

Ensign-George, Barry. "Denomination as Ecclesiological Category: Sketching an Assessment." In *Denomination: Assessing an Ecclesiological Category*, edited by Paul M. Collins and Barry Ensign-George, 1–21. New York: T&T Clark, 2011.

Eusebius. *The History of the Church from Christ to Constantine*. Edited by Andrew Louth. Translated by G. A. Williamson. New York: Penguin, 1989.

Farrar, F. W. *History of Interpretation: Eight Lectures Preached before the University of Oxford in the Year 1885*. London: Macmillan, 1886.

Fee, Gordon. *The First Epistle to the Corinthians*. Rev. ed. New International Commentary on the New Testament. Grand Rapids: Eerdmans, 2014.

———. *Pauline Christology: An Exegetical-Theological Study*. Peabody, MA: Hendrickson, 2007.

Ferguson, Everett. *The Rule of Faith: A Guide*. Eugene, OR: Cascade, 2015.

Fishbane, Michael. *Biblical Interpretation in Ancient Israel*. Oxford: Clarendon Press, 1988.

Foster, Douglas A. "Christology in the Stone-Campbell Movement: An Exploratory Survey." Paper presented at Restoration Theological Fellowship, Boston, November 20, 1999.

Gadamer, Hans-Georg. *Truth and Method*. 2nd ed. Edited and translated by Joel Weinsheimer and Donald G. Marshall. Bloomsbury Revelations. London: Bloomsbury Academic, 2013.

George, Timothy. *Reading Scripture with the Reformers*. Downers Grove, IL: InterVarsity Press Academic, 2011.
Gorman, Michael J. *Apostle of the Crucified Lord: A Theological Introduction to Paul and His Letters*. Grand Rapids: Eerdmans, 2004.
Gregory, Brad S. *The Unintended Reformation: How a Religious Revolution Secularized Society*. Cambridge, MA: Harvard University Press, 2012.
Gregory of Nazianzus. *On God and Christ: The Five Theological Orations and Two Letters to Cledonius*. Translated by Frederick Williams and Lionel Wickham. Popular Patristics. Crestwood, NY: St. Vladimir's Seminary Press, 2002.
Hanhart, Robert, Werner Kappler, Udo Quast, Alfred Rahlfs, John William Wevers, and Joseph Ziegler, eds. *Septuaginta: Vetus Testamentum Graecum*. Göttingen: Vandenhoeck & Ruprecht, 1931–.
Harrell, David Edwin. "Epilogue." In *The American Quest for the Primitive Church*, edited by Richard T. Hughes, 239–45. Chicago: University of Illinois Press, 1988.
Hicks, John Mark. "Theological Orientation for Churches of Christ: Resourcing Alexander Campbell's Trinitarian *Christian System*." *Christian Studies* 28 (2016): 21–36.
Holifield, E. Brooks, and Sidney E. Mead. "Puritan and Enlightenment Primitivism: A Response." In *The American Quest for the Primitive Church*, edited by Richard T. Hughes, 69–77. Chicago: University of Illinois Press, 1988.
Hughes, Richard T. "Introduction: On Recovering the Theme of Recovery." In *The American Quest for the Primitive Church*, ed. Richard T. Hughes, 1–15. Chicago: University of Illinois Press, 1988.
———. *Reviving the Ancient Faith: The Story of Churches of Christ in America*. 1996. Abilene, TX: Abilene Christian University Press, 2008.
———, ed. *The American Quest for the Primitive Church*. Chicago: University of Illinois Press, 1988.
Irenaeus. "Against Heresies." In *The Apostolic Fathers, Justin Martyr, Irenaeus*, edited by Alexander Roberts, James Donaldson, and A. Cleveland Coxe, 315–578. Ante-Nicene Fathers 1. Buffalo: Christian Literature, 1885.
———. *Against Heresies*. Translated by Dominic J. Unger. Ancient Christian Writers 55. New York: Newman, 1992.

———. *On the Apostolic Preaching*. Translated by John Behr. Crestwood, NY: St. Vladimir's Seminary Press, 1997.

Jeanrond, Werner G. *Theological Hermeneutics: Development and Significance*. New York: Crossroad, 1991.

Jenson, Robert W. *Canon and Creed*. Interpretation. Louisville: Westminster John Knox Press, 2010.

———. *Visible Words*. Philadelphia: Fortress, 1978.

Johnson, Edward. *Wonder-Working Providence of Sions Saviour in New England*. Edited by J. Franklin Jameson. Original Narratives of Early American History. New York: Scribner, 1910.

Jones, L. Gregory. *Embodying Forgiveness: A Theological Analysis*. Grand Rapids: Eerdmans, 1995.

Kelly, J. N. D. *Early Christian Creeds*. 3rd ed. 1972. London: Continuum, 2011.

Kemp, Anthony. *The Estrangement of the Past: A Study in the Origins of Modern Historical Consciousness*. Oxford: Oxford University Press, 1991.

Koch, Dietrich-Alex. *Die Schrift als Zeuge des Evangeliums: Untersuchungen zur Verwendung und zum Verständnis der Schrift bei Paulus*. Beiträge zur historischen Theologie 69. Tübingen: Mohr Siebeck, 1986.

Kraus, Hans-Joachim. *Psalms 1–59*. Translated by Hilton C. Oswald. Continental Commentaries. Minneapolis: Fortress, 1993.

———. *Psalms 60–150*. Translated by Hilton C. Oswald. Continental Commentaries. Minneapolis: Fortress, 1993.

Kruger, Michael J. *The Question of Canon: Challenging the Status Quo in the New Testament Canon Debate*. Downers Grove, IL: InterVarsity Press Academic, 2013.

LaCugna, Catherine Mowry. *God for Us: The Trinity and Christian Life*. San Francisco: HarperSanFrancisco, 1991.

Lasine, S. "Reading Jeroboam's Intentions: Intertextuality, Rhetoric and History in 1 Kings 12." In *Reading between Texts: Intertextuality and the Hebrew Bible*, edited by D. N. Fewell, 133–52. Louisville: Westminster John Knox Press, 1992.

Lawson, Stephen. "Historical Theology and the Stone-Campbell Movement." *Restoration Quarterly* 60, no. 1 (2018): 41–48.

Leith, John H. *Creeds of the Churches*. 3rd ed. Louisville: John Knox Press, 1982.

Lemaire, A. "Prières en temps de crise: Les inscriptions de Khirbet Beit Lei." *Revue Biblique* 84 (1976): 558–68.

Leuchter, Mark. "Jeroboam the Ephratite." *Journal of Biblical Literature* 125 (2006): 51–72.

Levenson, Bernard. "The Human Voice in Revelation: The Problem of Authority in Biblical Law." In *Innovations in Religious Traditions: Essays in the Interpretation of Religious Change*, edited by M. A. Williams, C. Cox, and M. S. Jaffee, 35–72. Berlin: Mouton de Gruyter, 1992.

Licona, Michael R. *The Resurrection of Jesus: A New Historiographical Approach*. Downers Grove, IL: InterVarsity Press, 2010.

Locke, John. *Second Treatise of Government*. Edited by C. B. Macpherson. Indianapolis: Hackett, 1980.

Luther, Martin. *Augsburg Confession*. Translated by R. Kolb, T. Wengert, and C. Arand. Minneapolis: Augsburg Fortress, 2000.

———. *The Book of Concord: The Confessions of the Evangelical Lutheran Church*. Edited by Robert Kolb and Timothy J. Wengert. Translated by Charles P. Arand. Minneapolis: Augsburg Fortress, 2000.

———. "Concerning the Letter and the Spirit." American ed. Edited by Jaroslav Pelikan and Helmut Lehman, 175–203. Luther's Works 39. St. Louis: Concordia, 1970.

Lyon, Gregory B. "Baudouin, Flacius, and the Plan for the Magdeburg Centuries." *Journal of the History of Ideas* 64, no. 2 (2003): 253–72.

Malherbe, Abraham. "New Testament Creeds and Their Uses." *Christian Studies* 14 (1994): 5–18.

Mandell, Alice, and Jeremy D. Smoak. "Reconsidering the Function of Tomb Inscriptions in Iron Age Judah: Khirbet Beit Lei as a Test Case." *Journal of Ancient Near Eastern Religions* 16 (2016): 192–245.

Marcos, Natalio Fernández. *The Septuagint in Context: Introduction to the Greek Version of the Bible*. Translated by Wilfred G. E. Watson. Leiden: Brill, 2000.

Martyr, Justin. *The First and Second Apologies*. Translated by Leslie William Barnard. New York: Paulist, 1997.

McClendon, James Wm., Jr. *Ethics: Systematic Theology*. Vol. 1. 2nd ed. Nashville: Abingdon, 2002.

McDonnell, Kilian. *The Baptism of Jesus in the Jordan: The Trinitarian and Cosmic Order of Salvation*. Collegeville, MN: Liturgical, 1996.

Miller, Herbert Dean. "Enacting Theology, Americanism, and Friendship: The 1837 Debate on Roman Catholicism between

Alexander Campbell and Bishop John Purcell." PhD diss., University of Dayton, 2015.

Miller-McLemore, Bonnie J. *Also a Mother: Work and Family as Theological Dilemma.* Nashville: Abingdon, 1994.

Moberg, D. O. "Denominationalism." In *Dictionary of Christianity in America*, edited by Daniel G. Reid, 350–52. Downers Grove, IL: InterVarsity Press, 1990.

Mommsen, Theodore E. "Petrarch's Conception of the 'Dark Ages.'" *Speculum* 17, no. 2 (1942): 226–42.

Morgan, Peter. "Five Finger Exercise." In *Encyclopedia of the Stone-Campbell Movement*, edited by Paul M. Blowers, Anthony L. Dunnavant, Douglas A. Foster, D. Newell Williams, 338–39. Grand Rapids: Eerdmans, 2004.

Murphy-O'Connor, Jerome. "Tradition and Redaction in 1 Cor 15:3–7." *Catholic Biblical Quarterly* 43, no. 4 (1981): 582–89.

Na'aman, N. "The Israelite-Judahite Struggle for the Patrimony of Ancient Israel," *Biblica* 91 (2010): 1–23.

Nelson, Janet. "Kingship and Empire." In *The Cambridge History of Medieval Political Thought, c. 350–c. 1450*, edited by J. H. Burns, 211–51. Cambridge: Cambridge University Press, 1988.

Nestle, Eberhard, Erwin Nestle, Kurt Aland, and Barbara Aland, eds. *Novum Testamentum Graece*. 28th ed. Stuttgart: Deutsche Bibelgesellschaft, 2013.

Neusner, Jacob. *Rabbinic Literature and the New Testament: What We Cannot Show, We Do Not Know*. 1994, repr., Eugene, OR: Wipf & Stock, 2004.

Newman, John Henry. *Arians of the Fourth Century*. 1833. London: Longmans, Green, & Company, 1897.

Newman, John Henry Cardinal. *An Essay on the Development of Christian Doctrine*. 6th ed. Notre Dame, IN: University of Notre Dame, 1989.

Noonan, John T., Jr. *A Church That Can and Cannot Change*. Notre Dame, IN: University of Notre Dame, 2005.

O'Brien, Mark A. "The Dynamics of the Golden Calf Story (Exodus 32–34)." *Australian Biblical Review* 60 (2012): 18–31.

Olbricht, Thomas. "Dispensations." In *The Encyclopedia of the Stone-Campbell Movement*, edited by Douglas A. Foster, Anthony L. Dunnavant, Paul M. Blowers, and D. Newell Williams, 28–83. Grand Rapids: Eerdmans, 2004.

Origen. *Contra Celsum*. Translated by Henry Chadwick. Cambridge: Cambridge University Press, 1980.

Pannenberg, Wolfhart. *Basic Questions in Theology: Collected Essays*. Vol. 1. Translated by George H. Kehm. Philadelphia: Fortress, 1970.

Parker, Kenneth. "Coming to Terms with the Past: The Role of History in the Spirituality of John Henry Newman." In *Newman and Life in the Spirit: Theological Reflection on Spirituality for Today*, edited by John R. Connolly and Brian Hughes, 51–74. Minneapolis: Fortress, 2014.

Pelikan, Jaroslav. *The Christian Tradition: The Emergence of the Catholic Tradition (100–600)*. Chicago: University of Chicago Press, 1971.

———. *Credo: Historical and Theological Guide to Creeds and Confessions of Faith in the Christian Tradition*. New Haven, CT: Yale University Press, 2003.

Petrarch. *De sui ipsius et multorum ignorantia*. Edited by M. Capelli. Paris, 1906. Translated by and quoted in Mommsen, "Petrarch's Conception of the 'Dark Ages.'" *Speculum* 17, no. 2 (1942): 226–42.

Porter, Stanley E. *Idioms of the Greek New Testament*. 2nd ed. Biblical Languages: Greek 2. Sheffield: Sheffield Academic Press, 1999.

Price, H. H. *Belief*. Muirhead Library of Philosophy. London: Allen & Unwin, 1969.

Rausch, David A., and Carl Hermann Voss. *Protestantism—Its Modern Meaning*. Philadelphia: Fortress, 1987.

Robertson, A. T., and Alfred Plummer. *A Critical and Exegetical Commentary on the First Epistle of St Paul to the Corinthians*. 2nd ed. International Critical Commentary. 1914, repr., Edinburgh: T&T Clark, 1929.

Robinson, J. A. T. "The One Baptism as a Category of New Testament Soteriology." *Scottish Journal of Theology* 6 (1953): 257–74.

Sampley, J. Paul. *Walking between the Times: Paul's Moral Reasoning*. Minneapolis: Fortress, 1991.

Sanders, Seth L. *The Invention of Hebrew*. Urbana: University of Illinois Press, 2009.

Schaff, Philip. *What Is Church History? A Vindication of the Idea of Historical Development*. Philadelphia: Lippincott, 1846.

Schniedewind, William M. *How the Bible Became a Book*. Cambridge: Cambridge University Press, 2005.

Silano, Giulio. "Introduction." In Peter Lombard, *The Sentences, Book 1: The Mystery of the Trinity*. Translated by Giulio Silano, vii–l. Toronto: Pontifical Institute of Mediaeval Studies, 2007.

Simons, Menno. *The Complete Works of Menno Simon, First Part*. Elkhart, IN: Funk & Brother, 1871.

Spieckermann, Hermann. "Barmherzig und gnädig ist der Herr . . . ." *Zeitschrift für die alttestamentliche Wissenschaft* 102 (1990): 1–18.

Stanglin, Keith D. "Apostles' Creed." In *Global Dictionary of Theology*, edited by William A. Dyrness and Veli-Matti Kärkkäinen, 59–60. Downers Grove, IL: InterVarsity Press Academic, 2008.

———. *The Letter and Spirit of Biblical Interpretation: From the Early Church to Modern Practice*. Grand Rapids: Baker Academic, 2018.

———. "Restorationism and Church History: Strange Bedfellows?" *Christian Studies* 26 (2013–2014): 21–32.

———. "The Restoration Movement, the Habit of Schism, and a Proposal for Unity." *Christian Studies* 28 (2016): 7–20.

———. "The Rule of Faith as Hermeneutic." *Christian Studies* 31 (2019): 7–15.

Stanley, Christopher D. *Paul and the Language of Scripture: Citation Technique in the Pauline Epistles and Contemporary Literature*. Society for New Testament Studies Monograph Series 74. Cambridge: Cambridge University Press, 1992.

Stark, J. David. "Baptism on Behalf of the Dead at Corinth—and in the Pentateuch?" In *Scripture, Texts, and Tracings in 1 Corinthians*, edited by Linda L. Belleville and B. J. Oropeza, 161–86. Scripture and Paul. Lanham, MD: Lexington, 2019.

———. "The Problem with Doctrines as Freestanding Assertions." *J. David Stark* (blog), July 15, 2019. https://www.jdavidstark.com/the-problem-with-doctrines-as-freestanding-assertions/.

———. *Sacred Texts and Paradigmatic Revolutions: The Hermeneutical Worlds of the Qumran Sectarian Manuscripts and the Letter to the Romans*. Jewish and Christian Texts in Contexts and Related Studies 16. New York: Bloomsbury T&T Clark, 2013.

Sterling, Greg. "Memory, Tradition, and the Future of Faith." Speech, Fourth Annual Abraham J. Malherbe Plenary, Christian Scholars Conference in Nashville, Tennessee, June 9, 2017.

Tabbernee, William. "Alexander Campbell and the Apostolic Tradition." In *The Free Church and the Early Church: Bridging the*

Historical and Theological Divide, edited by D. H. Williams, 163–80. Grand Rapids: Eerdmans, 2002.

Tannehill, Robert C. *Dying and Rising with Christ: A Study in Pauline Theology*. Berlin: Töpelmann, 1967.

Thiselton, Anthony C. *The First Epistle to the Corinthians: A Commentary on the Greek Text*. New International Greek Testament Commentary. Grand Rapids: Eerdmans, 2000.

———. *The Hermeneutics of Doctrine*. Grand Rapids: Eerdmans, 2007.

Thoreau, Henry David. "Walking." *The Atlantic*. June 1862. Accessed November 9, 2019, https://www.theatlantic.com/magazine/archive/1862/06/walking/304674/.

Toorn, Karel van der. *Scribal Culture and the Making of the Hebrew Bible*. Cambridge, MA: Harvard University Press, 2007.

Tyrell, George. *Christianity at the Crossroads*. London: Longmans, Green, & Company, 1913.

Vincent of Lérins. "Commonitory." Translated by Philip Schaff and Henry Wace. Nicene and Post-Nicene Fathers of the Christian Church, Second Series 11. New York: Christian Literature, 1894.

Voss, Hank. *The Priesthood of All Believers and the Missio Dei*. Eugene, OR: Pickwick, 2016.

Wallace, Daniel B. *Greek Grammar beyond the Basics: An Exegetical Syntax of the New Testament*. Grand Rapids: Zondervan, 1996.

Wamble, Hugh. "Landmarkism: Doctrinaire Ecclesiology among Baptists." *Church History* 33, no. 4 (1964): 429–77.

Widmer, Michael. "Moses, God, and the Dynamics of Intercessory Prayer." Durham Theses, Durham University, 2003. Accessed November 8, 2019. http://etheses.dur.ac.uk/3138/.

Widmer, Michael. *Moses, God, and the Dynamics of Intercessory Prayer: A Study of Exodus 32–34 and Numbers 13–14*. Forschungen zum Alten Testament 2/8. Stuttgart: Mohr Siebeck, 2004.

Wilk, Florian. "Isaiah in 1 and 2 Corinthians." In *Isaiah in the New Testament*, edited by Steve Moyise and M. J. J. Menken, 133–58. New York: T&T Clark, 2005.

Wilken, Robert Louis. *The Spirit of Early Christian Thought: Seeking the Face of God*. New Haven, CT: Yale University Press, 2003.

Williams, D. Newell. "Barton Warren Stone." In *Encyclopedia of the Stone-Campbell Movement*, edited by Paul M. Blowers, Anthony L. Dunnavant, Douglas A. Foster, and D. Newell Williams, 700–720. Grand Rapids: Eerdmans, 2004.

Williams, Rowan D. "The Body's Grace." In *Theology and Sexuality: Classic and Contemporary Readings*, edited by Eugene F. Rogers Jr., 309–21. Oxford: Blackwell, 2002.

Winthrop, John. "A Modell of Christian Charity (1630)." In *Collections of the Massachusetts Historical Society*, 3rd series, vol. 7. Boston: Little & Brown, 1838.

Wright, N. T. *The Climax of the Covenant: Christ and the Law in Pauline Theology*. Edinburgh: T&T Clark, 1991.

Wyclif, John. "The Wycliffite Bible: From the Prologue." In *Medieval English Political Writings*, edited by James M. Dean, 60–74. Middle English Texts. Kalamazoo, MI: Teaching Association for Medieval Studies (TEAMS), 1996.

Young, Frances M. *The Making of the Creeds*. New ed. London: SCM Press, 2002.

Zizioulas, John D. *Being as Communion*. Crestwood, NY: St. Vladimir's Seminary Press, 1985.

About the Contributors

Scott Adair is associate professor of Bible at Harding University. Adair has served on the faculty of the College of Bible and Ministry at Harding University since 2001. His current slate of courses includes Christology, Living Christian Traditions, Life and Teachings of Jesus, and Faith and Mission of the Church. He also serves as teaching minister at Highway Church of Christ in Judsonia, Arkansas, where he has been on staff for more than twenty-seven years. Whether speaking or writing, the topic of Christian unity through the gospel has been the primary focus of his ministry.

Stephen D. Lawson is assistant professor of theology at Austin Graduate School of Theology. He received his PhD in historical theology from Saint Louis University, writing a dissertation on the life and work of German theologian Erik Peterson (1890–1960). Lawson's writing has been published in *Logos*, *Modern Theology*, *Newman Studies Journal*, *Restoration Quarterly*, and *Stone-Campbell Journal*. His research is focused on theological responses to the rise of historical consciousness in modern theology, with a special interest in the intersection between theologies of history and political theology.

Daniel B. Oden is associate professor of Hebrew Bible at Harding University. Oden graduated from New York University's Skirball Department of Hebrew and Judaic Studies with a PhD in Hebrew Bible and Ancient Near Eastern studies in 2012. He has contributed to *A Comparative Handbook to the Gospel of Mark* (Brill, 2010), a forthcoming companion volume on Matthew and Luke, and an article in *Hebrew and Beyond*, a festschrift for Rodney Cloud. Oden's primary research interests are the Hebrew Bible, its reception in Second Temple Judaism, and the social world of the ancient Levant.

Keith D. Stanglin is professor of historical theology at Austin Graduate School of Theology in Austin, Texas, where he is the editor of the journal *Christian Studies* and the coordinator of the master's degree program. He has written or cowritten eight books, including *Jacob Arminius: Theologian of Grace* (Oxford University Press, 2012) and *The Reformation to the Modern Church: A Reader in Christian Theology* (Fortress Press, 2014). His most recent book is *The Letter and Spirit of Biblical Interpretation: From the Early Church to Modern Practice* (Baker Academic, 2018). He specializes in Reformation and post-Reformation theology, the history of biblical interpretation, liturgical theology, and Arminianism.

J. David Stark is Winnie and Cecil May Jr. Biblical Research Fellow at the Kearley Graduate School of Theology. Stark has published several articles and essays, as well as a monograph on how Paul read Scripture in his Second Temple context. Stark's research interests include how Paul and others in the early Jesus movement had their readings of Scripture shaped by their allegiance to Jesus and how some version of this reading strategy might be recoverable for the contemporary church. For more from Stark, subscribe to his website at jdavidstark.com, where he helps emerging scholars improve in the craft of working well in biblical studies.

Lauren Smelser White holds a PhD in theological studies from Vanderbilt University (2018). She also holds an MTS from Vanderbilt (2010), an MA in English from Abilene Christian University (2006), and a BA from Harding University (2004). White's scholarship attends to connections between interpretive praxis, systematic theology, and material culture. She is particularly interested in resourcing this work for the sake of generating constructive proposals in conversation with faith practitioners and theological educators. At Lipscomb University, White teaches various undergraduate and graduate courses in Bible and systematic, historical, and contextual theology. She and her husband, Jason, have two children.

Index

Ancient Authors and Their Works

Ancient Works

Modern Author Index

Scripture Index

Genesis

Exodus

Leviticus

Numbers

Deuteronomy

Isaiah

Jeremiah

Lamentations

Ezekiel

Hosea

Joel

Jonah

Micah

Nahum

Book of the Twelve

Matthew

Mark

Luke

John

Acts

Romans

1 Corinthians